The TRAIL
of
TEARS

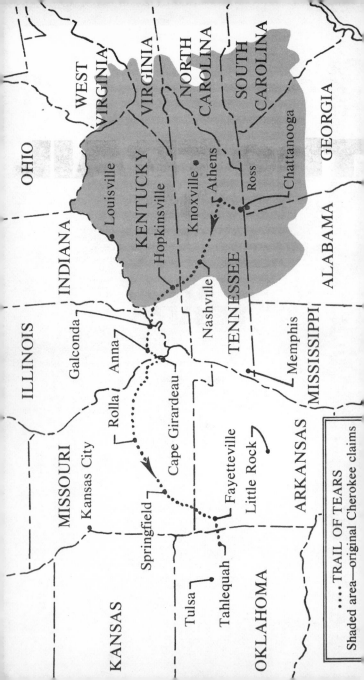

TRAIL OF TEARS
Shaded area—original Cherokee claims

The TRAIL of TEARS

W. A. Swonger

MOODY PRESS

CHICAGO

© 1976, by
THE MOODY BIBLE INSTITUTE
OF CHICAGO

ISBN: 0-8024-8797-1

Moody Press, a ministry of the Moody Bible Institute, is designed for education, evangelization, and edification. If we may assist you in knowing more about Christ and the Christian life, please write us without obligation: Moody Press, c/o MLM, Chicago, Illinois 60610.

Second Printing, 1977

Printed in the United States of America

1

John Ross relished the freedom his ancient buckskin shirt and breeches permitted; they were so different from the confining claw-hammer coat and tight pants his status dictated he wear each day.

But today he had been released from his responsibilities. The slaves needed a day off. Not him—Dad would never think of that! The *slaves* were tired. John grinned. Dad wasn't blind. He'd noticed how wearily John had trudged up to his bedroom last night.

Learning to oversee the Rosses' 700-acre plantation hadn't been as easy as he had anticipated. Sweat and guile were necessary to motivate the eighteen shirking slaves without resorting to whips. "Gain their respect. Show them you can do any job better than the best of them," Dad had ordered. "Make them hustle to keep up with you. Any slave worth his salt isn't going to let a gentleman attired in a suit outwork him. Makes him feel small."

He hadn't been certain he could obey those orders. But he'd stood in the loading line beneath the blistering sun for hours loading the heavy bales of cotton onto the flotilla of flatboats that were periodically poled upriver from the plantation to Chattanooga. Sometimes it had only been his pride that kept him going. Dad's sword had been two-edged; the gentleman in the suit couldn't quit with the slaves watching. Behind his back they would call him a lily-livered silk stocking. It had been satisfying when his soft, blistered hands had finally hardened. That had been months ago.

His training as overseer had sharpened his perception. The lean, hard-muscled youth rubbed an exploring hand across the back of his tanned neck. The short, fine blond hairs stood up sharply, giving him a prickly feeling of apprehension.

Sure got my hackles up this morning, he thought. *Since I found the landmark broken down, I've been expecting trouble.* The mighty boundary oak no longer securely guarded the east entrance to the Ross plantation. The giant tree had been hewed down, mercilessly mutilated by unknown hands.

John's deep blue eyes probed the countryside. The small lake sparkled serenely in the early morning sun. Across the lake, beyond scattered clumps of trees, the familiar rolling farmland stretched toward the distant foothills. Rising above the orderly row of hills were the mountains, following each other in a stately procession, their peaks shadowed with the ever-present smoky haze. Turning his back toward the thick forest, John stood tense, every sense vigilant to possible danger.

"Nothing seems amiss, but still I'll forego my swim this morning. I have to get home. Maybe our plantation's been put on the public lottery or another federal agent is trying to force us out."

In the hot, muggy air, John's moccasins made no sound. He walked with the springing, confident stride of one who is sure of his place in the world. The faint path he followed ran beneath trees festooned with ivy. The shrill chirp of an occasional bird, bees buzzing among wild flowers, and the whisper of squirrels' feet as they rustled about foraging for nuts were the only sounds.

A mother squirrel carried her baby across the trail toward a new nest. The squirrel hesitated, her baby dangling by the scruff of its neck in her careful mouth as she gazed inquisitively at the intruder. A fleeting smile tugged at the corners of John's mouth.

Despite the peaceful scene, a sense of urgency drove him. He broke into a trot. The humid air hung like a damp coat on his wide shoulders, darkening the buckskin.

"June 1838. Our time has expired. Two years the government allotted us to vacate. But we're not budging! Uncle John advised us to plant our crops, spin our cloth, and live as though nothing were wrong. Whites have flooded the country with whiskey, torn down our government, and converted our churches into grog shops. But the land is ours. President Jackson was well aware that the Cherokee treaty party that signed over the land was illegal. Less than one-tenth of the people

7

signed it." John swiped at the sweat beading his forehead. "I was born here where the wind blows free, and my father before me, and his before him. I know every stream and every wood." He dodged wild raspberry branches reaching across the trail to rip at his buckskins.

Suddenly a distant thunder of gunfire came from the direction of the house! John's feet pounded over the path. He shielded his face with his long arms as he plowed through the narrow opening between tangled branches, briars, and bushes.

Shot after shot crackled in the still morning air. *Must be an army of them,* John thought with a sinking heart. *Why didn't I bring my rifle?* The woods were thinning now. He ran hard, surefooted as a buck. As the acrid stink of smoke floated to his nostrils, icy fear clutched his heart. Breathing heavily, John sighted the house. A dull pain racked his side as he emerged from the woods. He dropped behind a large cucumber tree which hid him from view. What he saw sickened him.

The Ross mansion, grandly situated on a hill at the end of an avenue of stately oaks, was under attack. Puffs of smoke erupted from rifles dotting the perimeter of the stately white-pillared home. Bands of men took shelter behind well-trimmed hedges in the flower garden. By the confusion in their ranks, John could tell they were not trained soldiers. The Georgia militia, then; they looked more like bandits. The first summer flowers were being crushed beneath their heavy boots.

Deadly gunfire, originating from behind a dozen shade trees, peppered an upstairs window. One man had been driven behind the nymph in the fountain, getting his rifle wet in the process. A movement turned John's attention to the wide veranda encircling the house. A man crouched beside the parlor window. A tiny spark flickered, igniting a bundle of twisted straw. A faint tinkling of glass, and the blazing straw was inside. John gripped the trunk of the tree, murderous hate filling his heart. "Suicide to go out there!" Thick smoke billowed from the lower windows of the beautiful structure, blackening the fresh, white boards. Someone from an upstairs window was answering the gunfire. Through the smoky haze John saw a lone gunman frantically trying to reload.

For an instant John's father was outlined against the window, his grimly determined face gleaming palely through the smoke. Fire spurted from the guns below. Elias Ross clutched his head with both hands, then fell forward through the open window. His body hurtled through space, landing with a thud of finality on the lush grass.

Recklessly John bolted to his father's side, heedless of the soldiers. Dropping to his knees, he cradled his father's shattered head against his chest. Blood dripped unnoticed, spreading a dark red blotch on the gold buckskin.

John's voice was hoarse as he forced words through his agony-tightened throat. "Dad, can you *hear* me?" Staring in disbelief at what was left

9

of his father's head, a sense of utter horror transfixed him. His father's face was frozen in a look of perpetual surprise. John closed his eyes against the sight. His body shuddered with suppressed sobs. Hot tears forced their way between clenched lids.

Unnoticed, a soldier moved from the shadow of the veranda. As his rifle butt descended, pain exploded in John's head. Then darkness came.

Rough hands dragged John away from the burning building. Tongues of flame licked at the windows along the east wing of the house. Dumping the limp form on the gravel driveway, the soldier tied John's wrists tightly behind his back with rawhide thongs.

Drifting back into consciousness, his head aching with unbelievable pain, John caught scattered glimpses of the soldiers' relentless work. With their rifle butts, the looting militiamen had smashed in the windows, gaining entrance into the unburned portion of the mansion. Sooty-faced volunteers, dressed in anything from buckskin to broadcloth, and armed with ancient muskets, shotguns, pistols, and knives, made repeated trips into the flaming building, emerging with booty ranging from family heirlooms to copper spittoons.

Three husky men dressed in baggy homespun trousers and patched calico shirts strained clumsily at a rosewood spinet, managing only to get it firmly lodged in the now open front door. The devouring fire claimed the spinet.

Behind the pounding in John's head, a thought kept nagging. He groped, trying to shut out the pain, capture the nagging thought, and bring it into focus for examination. Something to do with the piano. What was it? Then the thought burst into his consciousness, boiling furiously with emotion so that he wished he hadn't found the answer. *The spinet is Mother's. Where is she? She was sleeping when I left this morning. I didn't see her come out of the house. Could she have gone out the back door while Dad was holding off the looters? No, they had the house surrounded. Is she still inside the burning building?* His thoughts made him struggle to his knees, but the effort only yielded a momentary return of the thick, soft blackness.

Then he could feel the intense heat from the burning building scorching his face, but dizziness obscured his view, or was it the thick smoke? Wavering figures, looking like specters in a nightmare, were scattering away from the house, heading toward the stables.

John's feelings were numbed now. What his mind recorded no longer registered on his emotions. It was as though he were somebody else, standing cool and remote above the still form lying in the driveway. He wondered vaguely if he were dead and his spirit had left his body. He felt a sense of duty now to record as in a journal what the soldiers were inflicting on the Ross family.

The invaders were out of sight, but above the crackling of the fire and the crash of falling timbers, John could hear them.

11

"I git that there Jasper. Never did see no horse-flesh could beat thatun!" howled a voice over the tumult of voices.

There was the noise of frightened horses neighing and prancing. Then they were loose, galloping down the drive. They came thundering toward John, causing the ground to tremble beneath his head. In the lead, the chestnut broodmare fell, a bone from her left leg protruding grotesquely at an angle. She squirmed, screaming in pain, pawing the earth, unable to regain her feet. The next few horses jumped over her, but the others, following too closely, trampled her. Her screams haunted John.

He felt the first two horses pass him with a sudden rush of wind and sharp pebbles striking his body. In a lucid moment he clearly saw the sweat streaming down the legs of the horses as they galloped frighteningly close.

Greedy men braved being stampeded to rope themselves a blooded horse. Elias Ross had owned some of the fastest horses in Georgia; the conquerors were not going to let them escape. Nor did they. Within minutes every horse had been captured. The black stallion named Jasper had two wild men fighting for possession. No holds barred, they were biting, kicking, and gouging one another. While the two rolled in the red clay, clawing for each other's eyes, a third man slyly leaped upon the quarter horse and headed for the woods.

A flying spark landed on John's back, burning through the buckskin, searing his flesh. The air had become so hot it scorched his lungs with each breath. More sparks touched his flesh like branding irons. He jerked his hands, but the tight thongs only cut into his wrists. He struggled to his knees, but the dizzy blackness returned. Collapsing, he rolled. The grass was singed, hard and prickly against his body. He rolled until he felt the pressure of a tree against his back. Here the grass was soft, the shade cooling. Resting his pounding head against the lush green carpet, he watched the gruesome scene.

Shoving each other in their greed, the thieving mob sacked the fifteen identical wooden structures housing the Ross's forty slaves. The frightened Black women and children were dragged from hiding places to be almost torn apart by the pack.

A babble of voices merged and swelled, with a few loud enough to be distinct. "I'm gittin' me a slave gal. Take yourn hands offen her; I had her first. I git her iffen I got to rip her arm clean off! Leggo, 'fore I shoot you!"

A skinny, sly-faced man, brown greasy hair straggling down his shoulders, tore a crying Black infant from his mother's arms as another soldier dragged the woman onto his horse.

"Hey, Jake, what you want that chile fer?" called a nasal Southern voice.

"My ole lady hankers fer a slave, even iffin she got to hand raise it" came the reply.

John saw Mammy Jolene attempt to stand

against the mob. "If my man was here, you wouldn't be taken me nowheres."

"We got to them husky field hands 'fore we came here. Surprised 'em. They's tied up safe in them trees yonder. We done put our names on 'em wif our knives, so we did," a gleeful voice declared.

"Hollingshead, you git these here slaves housed up real good, so's we can git em when we git back. Rest of you men, c'mon. We cain't stay here all day," ordered the sergeant as he and one of his men came back to the smoldering ruins of the mansion.

The smoke cast a heavy shadow, turning the sky a dirty brown, almost obliterating the sun. The stench of charred wood, of scorched and burned matter pervaded the air. Flakes of soot floated thickly, settling in a thin layer over everything.

As though they were separated from him by a long, dark tunnel, voices echoed indistinctly before they penetrated John's dazed mind.

"Ho, Sergeant. What are we going to do with the lad?"

"Huh, he still alive? Git him on his feet. He'll be shipped to Oklahoma Territory with the rest of 'em."

"He doesn't look well." The soldier looked at John's red, streaming eyes, still bleeding forehead, and limp body.

"Dump some water on 'im an let's git goin'. If he don't git up, shoot him," snarled the sergeant.

"Won't git no medals from Gen'l Scott iffen we're late."

The shock of water in his face roused John. Looking up through a foggy film, he shook his head groggily. A searing pain wrenched a moan from his dry lips. Through the brilliant spray of a million spots dancing before his eyes, he could see the two soldiers.

"Listen, boy, I want you to hear this. This is from Gov'nor Gilmer, Georgia's finest." The sergeant took a folded piece of paper carefully from inside his butternut linsey shirt and read in a loud, pretentious voice: "'To Thomas J. Worthington,' that's me, boy, 'for meritorious service in the Georgia Guard, the plantation, Pleasant Acres, now owned by one Elias A. Ross, consisting of 700 acres of tillable farmland and forest. Signed, Governor George Gilmer, Georgia.'

"The deed's all legal and proper, boy."

Seeing the naked rage on John's face, he assumed a brisk, businesslike manner. "Up on your hind legs!" When John made no move to obey, the sergeant seized John's arm and dragged him upright.

The ground whirled and swayed beneath his feet. John would have fallen without the support of the sooty arm. His stomach churned. He fought down the nausea, feeling acutely embarrassed at his weakness in front of these men.

Helpless and angry, John took a last look at his home through smarting eyes. The smoldering ruins had been his home these nineteen years. A

15

flaming fire of hate flushed his mind with fever. Some day the governor of Georgia would pay for this day's work!

A few hours ago John Ross had been a wealthy Southern aristocrat. What had he done to merit this treatment by the United States government?

2

The only breach of law John Ross had committed was being born one-sixteenth Cherokee Indian. Any person with one-thirty-second Indian blood, living on Indian land in the states of Georgia, North and South Carolina, Tennessee, Kentucky, and Alabama was being driven across the Mississippi River to the unexplored land known as Oklahoma Territory, already the possession of the wild Osage Indian tribes.

According to Cherokee law, all land any Cherokee lived on belonged to the entire Cherokee nation. It could not be sold without agreement of the majority of the 18,000 tribesmen, under penalty of death. Each Indian made the land his own by right of labor.

These lands had been given to the Indians in a legal treaty by the United States government for eternity. But now the greed for gold and land had resulted in political piracy. An illegal treaty had been signed and was being enforced.

But John had never expected a nightmare like this! His face was pale beneath the tanned skin. His lips were set in a rigid line; his eyes blazed with fury as he surveyed the smoking ruins. The dying embers of the fire were no hotter than the smoldering embers of hate in his heart.

"Dang it. I sure did hanker fer thet big house of yourn, but this riffraff they call the militia don't obey orders!" Sergeant Worthington frowned darkly. Then he rubbed his balding forehead. "Too bad your ole man decided to fight. He'd still be alive if he'd a come along peaceable like. What makes a man fight when he know'd he cain't win? He must a know'd he was a gone gosling. Him fightin' the whole squadron. That's the kind of man a soldier can admire." The sergeant shook his head slowly in wonder.

A crushing loneliness gripped John like a vise. He looked with dull eyes at the only home he'd ever known, now a blackened hole between two ghostly chimneys. Wisps of smoke spiraled from glowing ashes like phantoms of what had been.

The aching void in his heart had to be filled. Without conscious thought, he again chose anger over depression. His outraged fury exploded. Worthington was staring at the black hole like a man under a wizard's spell when the blow fell. The parallel kick caught the shorter man full in the chest, knocking him flat. His mouth opened like a fish caught on a rock, sucking for air.

John stumbled off balance without the use of his arms, then rolled to the ground. He lurched to his feet, too late. The other soldier rammed him hard in the stomach with his rifle butt. John doubled, groaning, retching on the soot-blackened grass.

He couldn't focus his eyes. His heart pumped but he couldn't breathe. Seconds passed before his breath started coming again with agonizing pain.

"If it wasn't fer my orders to bring you in, you'd be sure as shootin' gittin' a bullit in your gut!" The sergeant rubbed his calico shirt with dirty hands, his face contorted with pain. "But hear me good, Injin; you so much as look like you're gonna try anything, and it'll be my pleasure to see to it you don't make it to the stockade!"

With a naked bayonet stabbing into his back, plus a loaded rifle aimed at his head, John was marched by the two soldiers down the long drive to the dirt road. "This lad's just like his father; doesn't know when to surrender," the other soldier commented.

Responding to a shrill whistle from their commander, the squad of approximately forty volunteers fell in, surrounding the prisoner. The men were all aware that the prisoner was Chief Ross's nephew.

After John had been walking for some time, he heard a young voice taunting him. "Ho, Ross, you don't look so high and mighty today. Matter of fact, you don't look any better than any ole dirty squatter on your land. How's it feel to be walkin' 'sted of ridin' that fancy black horse of yours?"

It was Jeb Taylor. His father and older brother had ignored the boundary between white and Indian land, staking out a homestead for themselves on Dragging Canoe's land about a year previously. Jeb had been trying to court Melissa Vann without success. John's gut hurt too much to pay any mind to Jeb.

"Jebby boy," a second voice said, "young Ross could still send Melissa's heart aflutter. Even covered with dirt, she'd likely choose that handsome face to your orn'ry one any day. And looka that there physique!" The man drew out the unaccustomed word importantly. "It's like comparin' a bull moose with a cow." The other men guffawed. Already excited, the good-natured ribbing struck them as hilarious.

"No man's gonna call me a cow," Jeb muttered as he stuck his foot between John's legs, tripping him. With a vicious thrust, he shoved his rifle against John's back, causing the youth to land heavily in the red dust. Jeb jammed his boot on John's neck, pinning him down. The dust filled John's mouth, choking him.

"Seems to me he looks more like a worm burrowin' in the dirt than a bull moose. If I cut off your tail, can you grow another?" Jeb's voice was savage. By now the squad was drunk with excitement. They liked a good show, whether it was a cockfight or a brawl.

"I'm bettin' Melissa'd still take Ross!" a voice egged Jeb on.

"Take your foot off the prisoner, you jealous puppy!" someone else ordered. "I don't cotton to any man being tormented when he can't defend himself. You want to vent your spleen, Jason Wooster is your man." Wooster was a small planter who worked his own land adjacent to the

Indian reservation. He was respected by most men for his fairness as much as for his strength.

Jeb quickly removed his foot, looking shamefaced, his hazel eyes downcast. "Sorry, Jase, seemed like a good chance to get even. A man can't offen even scores with a rich man's son."

"Help him up," Wooster suggested mildly.

"He can get up hisself."

"I said, help him up!"

Jeb couldn't ignore the threat. Grudgingly, he helped John to his feet. John shook himself and spat, trying to get rid of the dirt in his mouth.

Belatedly Sergeant Worthington, who had been enjoying the ruckus, took command. "Cut the funnin' now. We got to git to town afore dark. I want him walkin' in, not dragged."

John began to doubt that he'd be walking in anywhere if they didn't rest soon. He estimated that they had been traveling for about an hour, walking briskly through the spongy heat.

"Chow time," the sergeant called.

Gratefully, the soldiers halted. They lounged on the ground beneath shady trees, breaking rations out of knapsacks or pockets.

"My feet are swole so big I cain't hardly git my boots off," one man commented.

"Dratted flies. Pesky things just keep swarming on a man when he's sticky." The speaker whisked his floppy brimmed hat in the air, chasing flies as big as june bugs. He pulled his clinging shirt, dingy

21

with sweat, away from his body. "Must be 98 degrees in the shade."

"Yep. The air's so wet I don't know whether it's sweatin' or I am."

No one offered John food or water. He sank beneath a tree, unable to find a comfortable position for resting with his hands tied behind him. Each beat of his heart brought a fresh burst of pain in his temples. His body felt like one bruised mass. Was he the only one of the family to survive? He'd been aching to know since the fire had claimed Mom's spinet. Wooster was sitting too far away to ask. He searched the guards' faces for a friendly one. He knew Taylor wouldn't say, nor would the sergeant. Perhaps that boy—couldn't be more than sixteen—who'd been eating steadily, not saying a word, could tell him.

John spoke in a low voice, not wanting anyone else to hear, "Did you see my mother or baby sister?" He cursed his voice silently for trembling.

Before the boy could empty his mouth of food, the sergeant rudely broke in, "I didn't see nobody come outen thet house. When it started burnin', it was a tinderbox."

John cringed as if from a physical blow. He leaned back against the tree, feeling sick.

"If I ever find the rapscallion that set fire to thet house, I'm goin' to tar and feather him, after I hamstring him. I've been dreamin' of settin' up housekeeping in thet mansion for two years. Gilmer and me had a little deal—" The sergeant broke off abruptly as attentive looks came in his direction.

"Don't worry. They got out alive," a sympathetic voice whispered. "The pony soldiers took 'em down the Post Road to town." Opening his eyes, John saw the boy had edged quietly to his side. John smiled gratefully.

A soldier drank noisily from his canteen. Then he tipped the canteen over his head, letting the water splash through his sweat-matted hair.

John's tongue was large and fuzzy against his teeth. Bits of grit were still lodged in his dry mouth. Salty sweat dripped into his eyes. He tried to brush it away with his shoulder. *Mother's alive. The pony soldiers are regular army; they won't molest her.* John's relief only made his thirst more acute. In an effort to forget his need, he looked inward into the mirror of his memory.

How lovely Mother had looked the other night. Dad and he had been sitting in the cool, book-lined library, his favorite room, the only masculine room inside the house other than his own bedroom. The massive, brown-leather pieces of furniture were the only ones on which his six-foot frame fitted comfortably.

Mrs. Ross had entered the room carrying a tray of mint juleps and some iced cakes. In the light streaming from the chandelier of candles, her hair shimmered. She stood tall and slender in her silk dress of powder blue, the exact shade of her eyes. Her billowing skirt rustled softly over the imported Brussels carpet.

There was no mistaking that Charity and John Ross were mother and son. Their Scotch ancestry was pronounced. Charity had been born in Sutherlandshire, Scotland, where she had lived until moving to Virginia when she was sixteen. With their honey-blonde hair and brilliant blue eyes, both mother and son had an inborn air of superiority. They possessed a self-assuredness about whatever they did. It was not arrogance but confident trust in their own ability. Yet, they were not offensive. They also shared a mannerism of looking directly into a person's eyes, giving him their complete attention, making him feel that they sincerely cared. When either entered a room, conversation gained a sparkle, a glow that had been lacking. Charity Ross was fully aware of her impact on people; John was not. He loved to hear his mother speak and could perfectly mimic the soft Scotch burr that made her speech so charming.

The family had been sharing a rare evening alone. "Two more months, John. Are you excited?" Charity Ross didn't wait for an answer. Her silvery voice rippled on. "I shall miss you terribly. Please post me a letter every week. Christmas is too far away, so your father and I will take the public stage to Princeton for a visit before the holidays." She glided to John's chair. Her hand was soft on his cheek. "There's still so much that I want to teach you. It seems like only yesterday when you were hanging onto my skirt. Now look at you!" She looked proudly at John's six-foot frame stretched languidly in the overstuffed chair. From his expertly razored blond hair to his polished, pointed boot tips, he looked every inch the rich young gentleman. The wine-colored wasp-waisted coat so popular these days accentuated his broad shoulders and narrow waist. The fawn pants were as tightly fitted as fashion dictated. Above his snowy linen shirt the black cravat was tied with just the proper careless elegance. He looked strong and confident, already a man. Only the reckless light that shone in his eyes and the boyish smile revealed his youth. He cut a figure no man in the county could best. He was a McCormac all right.

Raising her drink in a toast, Mrs. Ross said dramatically. "To Princeton! Our son will storm your ivy halls, then you'll see what a Southern Scotchman can accomplish. May you never recover."

Smiling indulgently, Elias Ross answered, "John's not going to prove anything about Southern aristocracy at Princeton." He took a slow sip, then continued in a serious tone, "No, he's going to show those intellectuals at Princeton what a Cherokee has in him."

Setting her glass quietly on the marble mantle, Charity turned regally toward her husband, saying in a coldly confident voice, "Elias, John is not going to flaunt his minute quantity of Cherokee blood. We shall not discuss the issue again. John realizes that sort of thing can only hinder his social life."

"Your long-nosed Scottish ancestors aren't

25

anymore honorable than mine!" thundered Elias Ross, banging his fist on the highly polished end table, making the bright astro lamp jump. "Did you have a better house in Virginia? Did you own more slaves?"

"Now, Elias," Charity said softly. She well knew how to charm her fiery husband out of his quick temper. "We are both keenly aware that our home is the showplace of Georgia. It's as elegant as any in Virginia. If it had not been so magnificent, my parents would never have consented to my marrying you. I've been very happy here," she soothed, her smile sparkling.

"Hang your parents! I would have married you if I had had to kidnap you. Just makes life more congenial to have their permission." His voice was excited, but less angry.

Steel crept into Charity's voice as she said, "You married above your Indian heritage. Now let John."

John spoke impatiently, his long slender fingers tapping restlessly on the arm of his chair. "Mother, I'm every bit as proud of being Cherokee as I am of being descended from Scottish lairds. I wish you would forget it. A person should be judged by his own merits, not by his pedigree." The soft drawl held an edge of disgust.

John was tired of the old argument. After twenty years of marriage, his dad never failed to get angry when Mother tried to gloss over his Indian lineage.

Now look where that lineage had landed him. There was no glossing it over. To the United States

26

of America, he was a Cherokee Indian. An un-
wanted alien. He, along with all the other half-
breeds, full bloods, and whites married to
Cherokees, was being expelled from his ancient
homeland. Like snow melting before the spring
sun, *Unaka,* the white man, had forced the Indians
farther, then even farther off their own land, and
now finally they were exporting them. *We Indians
should have maintained more stringent immigra-
tion laws,* John thought, a flitting smile on his lips.
It was strange thinking of himself as an Indian. Up
to this point he had thought of himself as John
McCormac Ross, a young man comfortable in
both white and Indian worlds.

Sergeant Worthington, wiping his perspiring red
face, called the men. "Let's go. We've got a whole
passel of redskins to git."

Under the blazing afternoon sun, the soldiers
marched on, going from farm to farm collecting
prisoners. They were participating in a well-
organized roundup of all the Indians in Georgia.
The road to New Echota forked to the left. Worthington ordered half of his men to follow him down
the main road, while the other twenty militiamen,
with John in their midst, traveled the smaller dirt
road which meandered ten miles farther across
country before intersecting with the main road
again just a few miles outside of town. Worthington put Taylor in command of the splinter
group.

The first farm on Pine Grove Road belonged to
the Raincrows. Taylor ordered that John be

27

backed up against a tree with a bayonet thrust against his chest when they came within earshot of the log cabin. The troops deployed around the building, then burst through the front door. In a few moments they dragged an old man out into the sun. John hated to see Granddad Raincrow treated so roughly. The old patriarch was revered for his knowledge of the ancient legends. As a young Indian he had been a great warrior. Granddad blinked at the soldiers in bewilderment, then called a grandchild to translate the unknown English into Cherokee.

Granddad's voice sounded unnaturally loud in the hot, still air. Solemnly, with innate dignity, his brown wrinkled face impassive as his native Georgian hills, he knelt on the red clay dirt. His five grandchildren obediently slipped to their knees in front of him. In melodic Cherokee singsong style, Granddad prayed. John was aware that Granddad was not praying to the great spirit, but to the white man's God. Strangely, the troops were more gentle with the old man.

The irregulars moved on relentlessly. The procession marched along Pine Grove Road, following the road as it meandered through a large valley floored with long, rolling hills. Between fertile farms surrounded with post and rail fences were pastures of cows and horses, orchards with fruit beginning to ripen, cow barns, pigpens, poultry yards, and storehouses—all Cherokee property. The spring houses looked especially inviting to John, who thought longingly of their cool interiors filled with cold buttermilk, cheese, and fresh spring water. Patches of heavy forests stood here and there among the farms. This was Catoosa County, one of the richest in northwestern Georgia.

As the procession approached Mill Creek, Bill Raincrow and his son were sighted in their cornfield. The corn was high and in tassle, almost hiding them from view. Apparently the troops knew just where to search. Grimly, Bill laid down his hoe, even now obeying the command of his chief not to resist. His son was not so willing; his angry face revealed a desire to fight. Bill signaled him to surrender quietly. Sullenly, they joined the group of prisoners. Bill's small daughter slipped her hand trustingly into her father's work-hardened one. John wondered where Mrs. Raincrow and the twin girls were. Months later he heard they had been helping a sick friend and had been imprisoned in a different stockade. Bill never saw his wife and twin daughters again.

After crossing Mill Creek on the rickety bridge, they passed the new gristmill. Its immense wooden wheel paddled placidly in the creek, providing the power to turn the great stone grinding wheels. John's thoughts took a strange turn as they plodded past the mill. *Was the Cherokee nation the corn being ground into dust between the merciless millstones of the United States government and the Georgia government?* He shook his head to dismiss the depressing thought.

The house of Echohawk was only twenty minutes farther down the road. Yesterday their small son had died. The body of the tiny child was lying on a bearskin-covered rope bed, while his sorrowing mother prepared it for burial. When she was arrested, her child's body was left deserted in the cabin.

The Vanns' home was next in line. It was a two-story red brick colonial structure, white pillared with upper and lower verandas across the front. Standing on a hill, it overlooked the entire valley. The house was empty. The army had been unable to surprise the family or—John looked at Jeb's relieved face—they had been warned about the roundup. Leaving the prisoners well guarded, the soldiers sacked the house of any valuables small enough to carry.

John noticed that the carriage was missing from the stable. The Vanns had probably headed north to live as white people. They had very little Cherokee blood flowing in their veins, so after making good their escape from the Indian reservation, they would never be mistaken for Indians. Perhaps Dad would have done the same had John been home before the soldiers came.

Melissa Vann had been considered a good match for John by her parents. Although John liked the girl, he had never given her the satisfaction of knowing it. But he was glad Melissa had escaped. Rich young girls had always had a habit of paying social calls to his mother, hoping to find John home. John had no intention of settling on any one girl for many years to come.

The guards had spent a good deal of time at the Vann home; so they tried to hurry the prisoners down the road, but the small children made their progress slow. The children walked uncomplaining, although they were bewildered, hot, and thirsty.

Upon reaching the neat farmhouse, owned by the Widow Takatokoh, the prisoners were forced to hide behind the empty corncrib. After surrounding the house, two soldiers pounded on the front door, demanding that the family come out. Mrs. Takatokoh opened the door a crack.

"Surrender quietly and no one gits hurt."

Mrs. Takatokoh had been sick for a long time. The frail widow gathered her children to her knees and prayed. Then she strapped her small son on her back and patted their old family dog good-bye. Taking a little child by each hand, she walked away from her home. But the effort proved too great. Widow Takatokoh clutched her chest, then fell on the ground, gasping, "Now I have found where the brightness is. Through the narrow door I go. There is gladness." She died there, with her baby strapped to her back, a child grasping each hand.

Tall, sorrowing Mrs. Echohawk moved to the dead mother's side, removed the baby, then strapped him to her own strong back. She gathered the sobbing children into her comforting arms. "Last night I lost my son. Today I take three new ones. Come, children, we must leave."

The hot afternoon sun beat unmercifully on the

31

pitiful group of prisoners, waiting for their strength to fail. John longed to leave the dusty road and walk beneath the shade of the trees.

They approached the Chickamauga River. The guards were strung out encircling the group of prisoners. Downriver about seventy yards was a heavy strand of trees. Almost before the thought formed in John's mind, he had broken through the guard, arched into a dive, and plunged deep into the river. He heard the thunder of rifles crack as the water closed over his head.

3

Using his legs to propel him deep under the water, John headed downstream toward the trees. With his arms free, the swim to the shelter of the trees would have been easy. John figured that once he gained the trees he could elude the soldiers, head for the ancient refuge of his people deep in the mountains of South Carolina, and then find a way to rescue his mother and sister. If he could only reach the trees, he felt reasonably sure he could regain his freedom. But getting to the trees would be a risk.

His lungs were bursting, burning for air. Still he kicked. John's ears began to buzz, his head to tingle. In the murky water he couldn't gauge how far he had come. Dark spots danced in front of his eyes; he had to surface.

The first lungful of air brought relief. Shaking the water clear from his eyes he saw with a sinking heart that he had fifteen yards to go. The river was no longer his friend. It became shallow here, with not enough protection from the Kentucky long rifles some of the volunteers carried. He had to run for the trees.

A quick glance revealed a handful of men hot on his trail. John mustered his strength and ran zigzagging toward the forest. Immediately a hail from the bridge revealed his position to the pursuers.

John put all his remaining strength into that fifteen-yard dash. Was he living a nightmare? His legs were churning, but he didn't appear to be moving. The whole world was in slow motion except for the pursuing soldiers. His chest ached; each breath whistled through his teeth.

Rifles spurted fire. The ground behind his feet was plowed into furrows by the balls and bullets. A sense of elation flowed, tingling his skin; he had made it to the trees. A stinging pain in the leg, the belated whine of a ricocheted bullet and he was somersaulting through a thicket. He landed on his feet and kept going.

Behind him a soldier threw his discharged rifle to the ground and raced to catch him. "Burned him in the leg. Come on, men, he can't last long now!"

Jeb Taylor again!

John couldn't keep up the pace. The pain in his leg was forcing him to limp. His lungs were agonizingly short of breath. Just ahead was a deep ravine. With a final surge of energy he gathered his strength to jump, figuring that Jeb wouldn't chance the danger. But Jeb's body hurtled through the air. He caught John just beneath the knees in a bone-jarring tackle. Knocked flat, John tried desperately to kick free. Taylor sat on him, pinning him to the ground until two other soldiers arrived to help. John lay on the ground drained of strength,

34

feeling a hopeless anger. Freedom had been so close.

Back on the road, John could barely force one foot in front of another. He limped painfully. The wet deerskin shirt sagged on his broad shoulders. His eyes were glazed.

The heavy, rhythmic beat of the blacksmith's hammer clanging on the anvil sounded above the muffled feet of the procession as they entered the village of New Echota.

The choking dust of the road changed into the slippery rounded cobblestones of the town's main street. The Cherokee council house stood like a giant mushroom in the center of town. John had sat in on the council meetings with his uncle numerous times as representatives from the seven clans had met to legislate laws for their people. The nation, under Chief Ross's leadership, had patterned its government closely after the democratic government of the United States.

In neat squares around the council house were built the homes of Indians. Each house boasted a garden and an orchard, plus the indispensable hothouse.

The town bustled with people. The celebration of *sah, looh, stee, knee, heeh, stah, steeh,* the Green Corn Festival, was in progress. Forming a square in front of the council house was the traditional embankment of sand, inside of which the ritual dances were performed. At the four corners of the square loomed the punishment poles. Any person making a disturbance during a dance, which might continue for days in succession, was tied by the wrists to the punishment poles until the dance concluded. There was seldom a disturbance.

Inside the sand-banked enclosure, a young girl was dancing the Friendship Dance. Even in his weakened condition, John admired her beauty. She was that rare Cherokee, a full blood, her skin an elegant sun-toasted brown. Large black eyes, heavily shaded with long lashes, gave an exotic appearance to her face. Her nose was slender above full red lips, while her thick black hair hung down her back, reaching well below the waist. For the dance she wore the primitive chaste white doeskin. Her short blouse was attached to her soft doeskin skirt with long, engraved silver brooches.

Without warning, a tall, brawny, obviously drunk soldier whose uniform was badly wrinkled, staggered toward the girl. Lust was plain in his every movement. He seized the girl around her slender waist, forcing her into a slobbery embrace. She wrestled one arm free, then slapped him. He lurched drunkenly, blood spurting from his injured nose.

"I'll teach you dirty Injun to hit a white man!" he bellowed. Holding her close in a bearlike embrace, he dragged her behind the council house.

For a second John was rooted to the ground. Hot blood pumped in his veins. He had to help that girl! He couldn't just stand there and allow her to be violated by that bull! He tried to shoulder his way through the guards, but one man, sensing his intent, grappled him to the ground.

On the far side of the council house an authoritative voice thundered, "Soldier, take your hands off that girl! Your orders are 'no molesting.'"

Judging by the look of the chastened soldier, the command must have come from a man of authority. Perhaps General Scott himself. Walking carefully straight, a silly grin plastered on his broad face, the soldier returned to the prisoners, holding the girl tightly by the arm. He hiccuped. John could smell his foul breath reeking of whiskey.

The girl looked contemptuously at the soldier. Only the bright color in her cheeks and the pulse that throbbed in her throat betrayed the ordeal she had just come through.

The white people in town for the festival gazed curiously at the Indians, just as though they had never seen them before, as if some of them had not bartered with them and neighbored with them only the day before. The town wore a holiday atmosphere. The tired group of dusty prisoners had become the entertainment now that the festivities had been interrupted by the seizure of the Indians.

The troop herded the unresisting captives toward a well equipped with a windlass and a bucket. The lid of sawed boards was removed. The bucket creaked down and was pulled up, brimming with clear, sparkling water. The children crowded around the bucket.

John sank to the ground beneath the shade of an

ancient oak. He closed his eyes. The surrounding sounds began to recede into the distance. The ache in his head began to lessen as he surrendered to a deepening darkness. But a sweet, husky voice nudged him back. "You look like you need a drink."

Even before he opened his eyes John knew that voice could only belong to the beautiful girl in the white doeskin. She knelt close to his side, a gourdful of water in her hand.

With an effort, John wormed himself into a sitting position. She held the gourd to his lips.

"Now I know what a dying man who has been saved feels like."

"Do you? I wonder," murmured the girl. The undertone in her voice revealed she had a different meaning in mind from what he had.

"After I wash the blood off your leg, I'll bring you more to drink." Each word she spoke was a delight. She rolled his blood-soaked trouser leg up, then gently cleansed the wound.

"That's a nasty gash in your leg; looks like a bullet grazed you. And your clothes are badly torn. You tried to escape, didn't you?" Her look was admiring.

"That's right." John watched eagerly, as the girl refilled the gourd. Trying not to gulp, he drank it all. The girl's exotic eyes caused a strange sensation in the pit of his stomach. Goose bumps chased each other up and down his spine.

"Why are your hands tied?" she asked.

"The soldiers evidently consider me dangerous," John said with a short laugh.

"I should think so!" she said, her eyes sparkling. "You fought them?"

John's face darkened. "No, I didn't get the opportunity." He turned away. He didn't want to talk about his capture.

"My name is Rachael Whiteswan. I have seen sixteen summers. My clan is the Wolf."

"I'm from the Wolf clan too. Name's John Ross from Pleasant Acres."

"Oh!" gasped the girl. A blush colored her sun-browned cheeks becomingly. Her long eyelashes brushed her cheeks as she lowered her head shyly. "I didn't know. I mean, I couldn't tell." She looked at the bloodstained, wet deerskin he wore. "You're not Chief Ross's nephew, are you?" He nodded. Still not looking up, she quizzed, "You live in the lovely mansion on the hill above Lake Hiwassee?"

"*Lived* in the mansion; they burned it." John's voice was harsh with bitterness.

"Oh, I'm so sorry," the husky voice said softly. "I didn't—"

Her words were interrupted by the coarse shouting of Sergeant Worthington.

"Let's go, you vermin! That's long enough. Git in line," he yelled. "Come on, hurry it up; I ain't got all day." The sergeant had just arrived to make sure that the remaining Indians were safely locked in the stockade.

John found it difficult to adjust to being treated in such a degrading manner. The more he was derided, the more obvious became his attitude of superiority. For him, it was a self-defense mechanism. For the soldiers, it became a goad.

Obediently, the captives gathered children and family groups and formed into lines headed toward the meadow outside the town. With quiet dignity the Indians left New Echota.

John and Rachael walked together at the end of the line.

"Where are you from, Rachael?"

"Back in the hills, near Stony Rock Creek. I came to New Echota just for the festival. My mother taught me the Friendship Dance before she died. You know, there aren't many girls these days who know the steps." Her voice was not proud, just matter-of-fact.

"We were wrong to ever leave the Indian way of life. Warriors wouldn't have passively handed over their lands," John said. "Dad didn't let the army take our land without fighting." A wave of respect washed over him, soothing his bruised feelings as he thought of the courage his father had displayed. "Dad's courage is the only legacy he was able to leave me. They won't be able to take that away from me."

"Did they kill him?"

She was shivering in the hot sunlight, but suddenly he wanted her to know.

"Dad knew he couldn't possibly win; he was fighting alone. Not just a detachment of soldiers, but the entire United States Army. He fought with Uncle John in Washington for our rights under the Constitution, but nobody cared. Today he fought with his rifle and lost again.'' A thought invaded John's mind before he had his defenses up: *Was Dad right to fight?*

As though she could read his mind, Rachael asked, ''He would be alive now if he had surrendered, wouldn't he?''

John frowned and was silent.

Rachael whispered, ''I'm going to untie your hands. They're all swollen and bloody.'' She struggled with the knots unsuccessfully.

''There's a knife in my pocket,'' John whispered, excited at the prospect of getting his hands free from the painful rawhide which had become progressively tighter as it dried after his swim. Rachael tried to get the knife from John's pocket without anyone seeing. They slowed their walk, but she couldn't reach the knife. Finally John stopped and Rachael was able to grasp the knife. She began sawing at the taut rawhide thongs embedded in his flesh, trying not to cut him. When the thongs fell at last to the ground, John sighed. He flexed his shoulders and arms, trying to work the stiffness out. He looked with dismay at his hands, swollen twice their size, a strange-looking mottled color. His hands had lost their sense of touch, he discovered, when he took his pocketknife in clumsy fingers to return it to his pocket. The young volunteer who had told him about his mother was

41

watching them closely, but he made no move to interfere.

"How do they feel?" Rachael asked with concern.

"Can't feel anything now; they're numb. My arms and shoulders ache like I've been tortured on the rack. Thanks." John clenched and unclenched his hands, trying to restore the circulation.

"Dad wasn't the only one killed. A sick widow died because the strain of capture was too much for her. These men are ruthless. Look, Rachael, thanks for cutting my hands free, but you're going to have to be more careful. If anyone else besides that young boy noticed that knife in your hands, they might have killed you. They're not playing games."

His words of caution did not seem to have any effect on the young girl. She merely smiled mystically. Answering his puzzled look, she said, "God will not permit me to die until it is His will that I go to be with Him."

John shuddered. What kind of crazy talk was that? He had seen death come violently today. He had felt like his own heart had been torn out when he had seen his father fall. How could *that* be the will of God? Did this girl think she was immune to violence just because she believed in God?

Soon the two of them were walking beside Mrs. Echohawk and the three small orphans who had lost their mother earlier in the day.

One small boy began to cry. Rachael stooped

beside him to comfort him. "What's wrong, little one?" she asked.

"I want my mommy! I'm tired, and I just can't walk any farther," he sobbed.

"How about a horsey ride?" John said, grinning down at him. The boy smiled faintly through his tears. Despite his painful leg, John swung the child up on his back. Mrs. Echohawk gave him a grateful look, for she was still carrying the baby on her back, although the older boy was walking manfully at her side.

"What's your name, Chief?" John asked the child on his back.

"I'm Little Eagle. Sometimes Ma calls me Joseph." He snuggled his head against the back of John's shoulder.

"Little Eagle, you can ride all the rest of the way," John promised. The boy laughed with delight.

They could see the stockade about half a mile ahead, situated in the center of a large meadow. To the right was a thick forest. John felt a pang of depression as he looked at the newly built stockade. Not very large, maybe only a hundred yards long, it was constructed of split trees which had been sharpened and then set picket-style into the ground. On three sides of the stockade the army had pitched their tents in neat, parallel rows. "Looks like a city living under canvas. Those poor soldiers must be boiling hot in those tents during the day," Rachael pointed out. John found it impossible to feel any sympathy for the "poor soldiers."

It was dusk as the procession reached the stockade. Two armed men, who had been slouched on either side of heavy, double doors, quickly jumped to attention, the setting sun flashing on their guns. As one soldier lifted the heavy latches, John turned for a final glance at the freedom of the open country. A brilliant sunset of orange, purple, pink, and scarlet painted the darkening sky. The glow bathed the rolling countryside, tinting the earth where the sky and mountains met in a purple haze; it was distressingly beautiful. In the meadow, wild geranium, wild gooseberry, and trees entwined with wild grapevines taunted John with the freedom he was losing.

"The white man can imprison my body, but not my spirit," breathed Rachael.

Then they were inside. The massive doors swung shut behind them with a heavy thud. Two small crude enclosures, constructed of undressed logs chunked with clay, were built at either end. There were no trees. The hard red clay dirt, trampled beneath the feet of hundreds of Indians, was naked of meadow grass. The place was overflowing with people. Men searched for wives and children among the new arrivals. Babies squalled. Worried women with small children in tow were scanning the new faces to see if the children's mothers had been brought in. Other mothers were in panic looking for lost children. The noise was deafening. All levels of society were here, ranging from the very poor to the very rich. Some Indians were even dressed in nightclothes. Either they had been captured very early or very late and given no opportunity to dress. There were white, brown and red people, from the elderly down to the very young. The only identity the swarming mass of humanity held in common was a dazed look of bewilderment. John couldn't see his mother.

The sun slid below the mountains. As darkness fell, soldiers herded the men and boys into one building and the women, girls, and small children into the other. John was directed into the tightly packed men's building. There were no windows, and the stifling room was inky black. The odor from closely packed, perspiring bodies was nauseating. Men and boys settled on the hard-packed dirt floor. John stumbled over several prone bodies in the darkness before he found space in which to squeeze. A sick, dizzy feeling warned him to lower his head between his knees to ward off faintness. For once he was glad his stomach was empty; the way it was churning, he knew he would have vomited. What a dilemma that would have been. He would have had to sit in it; there was no place else to go. Judging by the smell, someone else had not been so fortunate.

Someone stepped hard on his hand, and John began to tremble, his last reserve of strength gone. The confinement was not bearable. Sweat poured from his body as the sea of noise slapped his defenseless ears and the stench filled him with nausea. The oppressive heat and the lack of space combined with his pounding temples was too much. He fought a rising panic. He had to get out!

"Overwhelming, isn't it? In a night or two you'll become accustomed to it." A friendly hand was heavy on his shoulder as a soothing bass voice rumbled calmly beside him in the dark. John's rigid body relaxed slightly. Contact with another human being who seemed concerned had a quieting effect. "They release us first thing in the morning," the voice continued. "The secret to adjustment is to stay calm and don't panic. Relax as much as you can—mind over matter. Take slow, deep breaths. You can overcome this situation. My name is Sam Worchester."

John felt his panic begin to subside. He forced himself to breathe regular, slow, deep breaths. In the darkness he could only see a dark lump sitting next to him.

"I assume you haven't eaten," Worchester said. "We receive our allotment of food at midday. Not very appetizing, but it should keep body and soul together." John's heart sank. He'd really been expecting to eat when they reached the stockade. He should have realized they wouldn't have a hot meal ready for him.

"Do you have any injuries, son?" Worchester's kindly voice probed.

"Yes, sir. I got a rifle butt in the head this morning. My head feels like it's going to explode. I got shot in the leg, too; must not be too bad, but it's painful."

"I have some herbs. We'll make a poultice with

46

my handkerchief and wrap it around your leg. Old Indian remedy. It'll help no matter how bad the wound. Did it bleed clean?''

"Yes, sir. My pant leg was soaked with blood.''

"Unfortunately I've used up my supply of other medicinal herbs or I could give you something for that head. I'll brew you some special tea tomorrow after the girls gather more roots for me,'' Worchester promised.

"I'm grateful for your help, sir. Are you a medicine man?''

The low, rumbling laugh made John think of pleasant times. "No, I'm about as far from being a medicine man as I can think of. I'm Reverend Worchester. Been a missionary to the Indians for the past five years. Was interested in their healing arts, so studied all I could in my free time. Pretty good remedies too. Without any hocus-pocus magic, I might add. Nothing mystical about the procedure. Just using the balms the good Lord provided.''

John felt a little strange. This was the second religious person he had met today and *liked*. Was this some type of conspiracy? His eyes were adjusting to the dim light. He could see a small man, slightly built, wearing a pair of eyeglasses perched on his nose. From the deep, rich quality of his voice, John had expected a larger man.

"About eight o'clock in the morning they open the stockade doors. Those who wish to do so may leave under guard to attend the worship service. We are permitted to sit among the trees. The girls

47

stay within earshot so they don't miss the sermon while they gather roots and herbs for medicine. I hope you will join us."

The persuasiveness in the man's tone had no effect on John. He just wasn't interested. Worchester could not help but hear the bitterness in John's voice as he declined, "No thank you, sir. I'll drink your brew, but—I don't mean to be rude, sir—but your God just isn't very believable after what I've been through today."

4

Drifting into John's awareness came the feeling that someone was watching him. Opening his eyes, he noted without surprise that the person stood exactly where his senses had pinpointed. Copper red hair gave the man a youthful appearance. Inquisitive green eyes peered through rimless glasses. "How do you feel this morning, young man?" Worchester asked.

John sat up and gingerly touched his head. Very gently he closed his eyes. The pain was fierce. The slightest movement awakened a new twinge. "Did you ever have a war party dance on you, sir?" he answered with a crooked smile.

He noted with surprise that they were alone. It must be very late. He squinted at the sun through the open door.

"You don't look any better than you feel. You have a nasty bruise covering your temple, extending down to your left eye." Worchester stood up as though his legs were stiff from squatting. "I got a bit concerned when you didn't wake. I thought it best to come in and check on you."

Carefully unfolding his long frame, John stood

erect. The bright head reached only to his shoulders. He liked Worchester and his warm personality.

"The girls brought in a mixture of herbs and roots this morning that I fancy will help that head of yours."

"That's most handsome of you, sir; I appreciate your concern."

Together they stepped through the door into the sunlight. The heat hit John like a physical blow. Feeling sluggish and out of temper, his mouth was as dry as the red Georgia dust. It tasted like the militia had marched through it last night, closely followed by the pony soldiers.

The stockade was quieter this morning. Most of the people lolled aimlessly. The high stockade walls closed in on John, creating an unreasonable urge to pace the enclosure—back and forth, back and forth—looking for a way of escape.

Other faces reflected different degrees of the identical agitation he felt. Worchester had a smile or word of encouragement for each person he passed. His was the only smiling face John saw. He led John to a campfire over which a steaming kettle hung from a tripod. John accepted a gourd filled with tea of a distinct odor, mildly pleasant. The taste was tart, just short of being bitter, but it was wet! Even before the gourd was empty, drowsiness began calming the caged-animal feeling. The sharp pain knifing into his brain dulled. John felt his taut nerves loosen, his knotted stomach relax. He watched Worchester leave on some other errand of mercy through a haze of light-headed relief.

Now to locate Mother in this throng. Most of the faces were those of strangers. A deep pity for these people compressed his chest. Had Uncle John been wrong when he had advocated no resistance? Perhaps the passive fatality of the Indian mind, which neither questions nor complains but loyally obeys the decree of its chief, had brought about its own destruction. But resistance hadn't been possible. There were few arms and no leadership. Even the war chief was committed to Uncle John's path.

"Where's your uncle, John?" A rough hand clapped him on the shoulder. Pain shot through his head. He turned carefully to find Jonah Water Spider frowning at him. He had never had much use for the spare little Indian with the whispy goatee. The man's dark eyes darted over John's hair, his moccasins, his left arm, but never met his eyes.

"Good morning, Mr. Water Spider. The last I heard, Chief Ross was still in Washington attempting to negotiate with the great father. He has in his possession a petition signed by a majority of the eligible brothers to the effect that our tribal lands had been assigned us forever by the white man's treaties. He hopes to prove that the signers of the removal treaty are guilty of treason." When speaking with the Indians, John often lapsed into their picturesque figures of speech.

"Yes, yes. I am aware of that. I also signed the

51

petition. I thought perhaps you had received a letter.'' His hand shook with agitation as he tugged at his beard. ''Perhaps we shall be released soon. Certainly the Americans won't hold us prisoners long. Someone has made a terrible mistake.'' John impatiently shifted his feet. He wanted to continue his search, but the older man continued. ''Yesterday's *Banner and Whig* was full of America's fear that some of the states would secede from the Union. There were fiery editorials on the slavery issue, but not a word about our problem. What can Chief Ross be doing?''

''Since President Jackson has wielded the power, Chief Ross has not had an open entrance with the great father. The new Democrats are still moved by Jackson's iron hand. I think, however, as long as Chief Ross remains in Washington we can hope for the release of ourselves and our land.'' John knew the hope was slender. A circle of listeners had clustered around them when Chief Ross's name had been mentioned. It was for them John withheld his true thoughts.

''Excuse me, I must find my mother. Have you seen her?''

Water Spider shook his head. He looked unconvinced but more hopeful.

As he searched, John recognized an acquaintance here and there. He shook a hand or made a bow. His heart grew heavier. Whites married to Indians had been imprisoned along with their spouses. No one on reservation land in his county that he was acquainted with had been spared.

There must not be a person with one drop of Cherokee blood walking free in Georgia today, he thought.

An unreasonable hope began to build itself into certainty that somehow his mother had not been brought here. Or maybe the boy lied. Maybe she had died in the fire. With mingled relief and disappointment, he saw her sitting in a narrow strip of shade against the log poles. At least she was dressed. No one looked more out of place than she. *I've never seen her sitting on the ground before.* John thought. *Not even on the lawn under the shade trees. A slave had always brought a chair.*

Dodging between irritable people, he wended his way to her. Even limping, John walked with an air of independence. His mother recognized that unmistakable stride and rushed into his arms.

"Darling, you look awful, but you are alive!" Holding her tenderly in his arms, John realized he had never done that before. It felt right. They had never been a demonstrative family. "Where's Pris?" he asked, his voice breaking like a young boy's.

"Rachael has her. I don't quite know how it happened, but last night in that awful place I met the one person who could give me some detailed news of you. Such a relief to know you were safe. I don't believe I could have survived last night without Rachael. She is a dear girl. Come, sit down, tell me all about what has happened to you."

Rachael joined them after a few minutes. She seemed a bit shy today. Priscilla was sleeping soundly, cradled in a shawl fastened beneath her and then draped over Rachael's shoulder. Rachael and Charity had evidently become close friends during the night. *They are a study in opposites,* John thought. *Mother is tall, blonde, her pale complexion like the petals of a white rose, looking fragile and helpless, but still that innate self-assurance is shining through. Rachael is tall, brown-skinned, competent but shy, looking very much a daughter of the land.*

Just then the familiar resonant bass voice of the small preacher, Sam Worchester, called, "Come, folks! Let us gather together for strength and encouragement from our Lord."

Rachael rose immediately, murmured to Charity, and followed the crowd to the gates.

"Please come, John. Rachael has told me some interesting things I had not thought of before. Besides, it must be much cooler outside beneath the shade of the trees." Charity's sky blue eyes looked up pleadingly.

John reflected on the lines of sorrow etched around her mouth where none had been yesterday. The soft chin was set courageously. He could not say no, even though his own heart was heavy and bitter against God. Gently John placed her slender hand in the crook of his arm as they followed the pressing crowd of people toward the open door.

The guard scrutinized the pair closely as they passed. He thrust his rifle rudely against John's chest, shoving him to a standstill. "The rule is you give your word of honor you won't try to escape!" he barked. John thought the guard looked like a coyote with his rather pointed ears, skinny face, and long nose. He kept his face impassive, looking over the guard's head toward the woods.

Charity's voice was haughty, the voice she reserved for gossipy females, "Certainly, we give our word. Our purpose is to hear the Reverend Samuel Worchester's message. That's why he is here in this overgrown pigsty. He is sacrificing his own freedom to minister to these people. Not many men have that nobility of character," she added pointedly.

The guard grudgingly lowered his rifle, allowing them to pass. John heard him mutter, "Don't like the looks of that breed. He ain't got all the fight beat out of him yet. He don't look to me like he's goin' to any church meeting."

Rachael's welcoming smile made John's heart hammer like a blacksmith on a hot horseshoe. They settled under some large trees. It looked as if all the people had come out of the stockade. *Bunch of sheep,* John thought with contempt. The slight breeze under the tree cooled his hot forehead, and he squinted in the glare.

Beyond the stockade, miles of mountains stretched on in triple peaks as far as his eye could see. He had never looked at those majestic peaks without a feeling of kinship; he had seen them every day of his life. He remembered the words, "Spirits of the mountains . . . worshiped by my

Cherokee ancestors in the dim days of antiquity. . . ." But he couldn't concentrate.

It was difficult not to listen to Worchester's compelling voice. A man with a voice like that should be in Washington persuading the government leaders.

John focused his attention instead on the soldiers. *So these are the soldiers that defeated Great Britain, the most powerful army in the world. They're not that impressive.* The soldiers were scattered over the meadow in such great numbers that it was impossible to see the edge of their bivouac. A lively horseshoe-pitching contest was in progress far to his left. The men were stripped to the waist, wrangling among themselves. Two broke away from the group to measure the distance between the horseshoes.

In the distance, John could faintly hear the voices of another knot of men wagering on the outcome of a wrestling match. He couldn't see the contestants, but the dust was swirling around the boots of the audience.

The army owned some beautiful horses. A bay Tennessee walking horse, with his rocking-chair gait, proudly carried his master on some errand. Four matched Morgan horses were tethered near some light howitzers. What the army was planning to do with those guns John couldn't imagine. *Looks like an entire regiment of artillery camped over there,* he thought, his eyebrows raised in surprise. He watched with interest as a gun crew swabbed out the cannon, then rammed in a new charge. They used almost a full powder horn of gunpowder in the iron gun.

A pale Arabian horse galloped by, flanks lathered in the heat. "Drinkers of the Wind," the Arabs called them. *That jackass riding her like that in this heat must be one of those saddle boys from Washington; all political pull and no practical experience,* John mused.

"But he was wounded for our transgressions, he was bruised for our iniquities."* The words Worchester spoke penetrated John's mind before he closed his ears again.

Stockade's solidly built. Must be about ten feet tall. They pointed the spars. No visible break in the wall. No other guards posted except at the gate. They must be pretty confident it's escape proof, he thought.

About fifty feet on this side of the stockade the Conasauga River splashed its way into the thick forest. The sound of the tumbling waters whispered softly below Worchester's melodic bass voice. Near the river many girls were gathering the yarrow which he knew would be used to repel chiggers and gnats. Others were picking wild lettuce, mustard greens, and wild onions. What else they were finding he couldn't even guess. The girls were difficult to see, stooped among the tall grasses, but none was as lovely as Rachael. If she had a physical flaw, he hadn't detected it. John wondered how long men were to be imprisoned so

*Isaiah 53:5

57

closely with women before the lines of convention and morals would be crossed. One more added agony!

The mountain laurel, wild indigo, crape myrtle, and wild azalea were thick by the river. If the heat was not so intense and his stomach so empty and that voice so utterly annoying, he could enjoy the scene. It was certainly colorful. He glanced at his mother's face. She was staring intently at Worchester, her chin cupped in her hand as though making an evaluation. John had always admired his mother's quick, logical mind. If she was so engrossed, the man must be saying something worthwhile.

"He was oppressed, and he was afflicted, yet he opened not his mouth."† The anger lying very close to the surface of John's soul began to fan into flames.

"He is brought as a lamb to the slaughter, and as a sheep before her shearers is dumb, so he openeth not his mouth."‡

John felt the words burn into his heart. Unconsciously, he clenched his fists, and the taut muscles rippled over his set jaw. *That's just what the white man did to us! Stupid sheep. Ridiculous to submit passively.* He jerked violently to his feet. Mother and Rachael gaped at him in astonishment. He strode away from the listening group, intense anger evident in his every movement.

He had not intended to cause a scene or even to

† Isaiah 53:7a
‡ Isaiah 53:7b

get up and leave, but the strong emotions chafing inside him had to have an outlet. He headed for the thick woods, turning back at just the last minute. *Of course we shall not try to escape,* echoed in his mind. *I can't bring dishonor to Mother. What would they do to her if I ran? Besides, the woods are probably bristling with soldiers.* John stopped abruptly. As he grimly turned to go back toward the stockade, he saw a flash of light reflected from the barrel of a gun. *That sharpshooter had me sighted,* he realized. *He would have shot me down like a dog.* John's heart pounded and his stomach tightened into a hard knot. *The coyote looks disappointed. He really wanted to shoot me!* Trying to appear cool, John quipped to the guard as he reentered the prison, "Sorry to disappoint you. No target practice today."

"Tarnation! Not today, but I'm waiting. The only good Indian is a dead one" came the insulting answer. John held his head higher, trying to dispel the feeling of degradation the words conveyed. The stigma of being an Indian was rubbing his feelings raw. It was a strange new experience being treated as less than human. He knew the difficulty was to remain objective and not to see himself in that light.

Inside, the stockade was blazing hot and empty. No breeze whispered through those tightly picketed poles. *Not a soul here.* John wished his temper were not so fiery. Just like Dad's. *I could be out sitting under the trees. This place is an inferno.* John's body was sticky with sweat. Flies swarmed over to light on him, adding to his irritation. The prison was full of flies. The United States government had provided no sanitary facilities. *They can't intend to keep us here long,* John thought with repulsion.

Walking over to the women's building to inspect it, he found it be identical to the men's, only it smelled worse. *Must be the children. Somehow I have to get Mother out of here!* He kicked a board in frustration. As a huge rat scuttled away, a shiver of revulsion skipped down his backbone.

The sound of moccasins muffled in dust like so many faraway drums beating plaintively signaled that the other prisoners were returning. Hundreds of Indians straggled slowly back into the ovenlike stockade. John saw many faces he recognized, but the vast majority were strangers.

A pair of oxen dragging a heavily laden wagon followed the Indians inside. "Line up by families, you filthy redskins," bellowed a heavily muscled soldier. "Git your grub and water." John recognized him immediately as the man who had attempted to assault Rachael. The man's thick neck, his large head bristling with dark hair, made him look very much like a bull. Standing with his legs spread apart on top of the supply wagon, he waited impatiently for the family groups to form into a line for their daily dole of food.

The wagon master's unintelligent gray eyes smoldered beneath a scowl until he spied Rachael. She stood alone, the profanity in his eyes making her blush. "You ain't got no family, girl, so you

60

don't eat," he called to her in a gloating voice. "Unless you're nice to me!"

John's blue eyes blazed, then turned cold, as steel glinted in their depths. Looking squarely into the wagon master's ugly face, John spoke quietly, the slow accent of the Georgian highlands converted into a sharp, crisp staccato which an overseer uses with a clumsy field hand. "The girl is my sister by clan bonds. I am responsible for her. Don't you ever make the mistake of touching her. I know General Scott's orders. I'll see to it you are court-martialed if you break those rules."

The wagon master's face turned crimson, then a sickly yellow. He took a step forward as though he intended to jump down from the wagon and tear the young man apart limb from limb. Instead, he gripped his hands behind his back, as though physically restraining himself. He muttered, "Git in line then, Injin." John's food supplies were thrown in the red dirt at his feet. Water was sullenly ladled into a bucket, which was then thrust into his hand with such force that a quarter of its contents spilled. The tiny puddle of water was instantly sucked into the dry red dust. John heaved the small burlap bag of food over his shoulder. Carrying the bucket in his free hand, he motioned with a nod of his head toward Rachael, his mother, and Priscilla. Together they sauntered around the men's building to get away from the livid eyes of the wagon master.

Gratitude radiated from Rachael's black eyes. Charity looked worried. "John, please stay away from that horrible man," she pleaded. "You've been a champion to the helpless since you've been old enough to understand need. I'm pleased you were able to come to Rachael's aid, but you must learn to be less reckless. I'm sure there must have been other men who would have stood up for her." She looked uneasily at the crowd of prisoners. Then the worried look faded. A gentle smile so like Priscilla's transformed her face. "I well recall the first time you displayed this facet of your personality. You were barely four. Three of our pickaninnies were tormenting a fighting cock your father had penned. You wouldn't permit that kind of treatment. You stood there like a little cock yourself among those older children and made them stop. Your father laughed when I told him that night. He said you'd put your saddle on the other horse when you became old enough to bet on a cockfight. But he was wrong. How many scrapes you got into after that! You never learned to stay out of a problem when an injustice was being committed. That's why your father thought you would make a fine lawyer." Charity Ross's voice had been almost gay as she recalled the younger days at Pleasant Acres, but it ended in a sob.

Pastor Worchester put a kind hand on Mrs. Ross's arm. Then he placed her hand through his arm, walking companionably with her. John hadn't seen him arrive. The man had an uncanny knack of springing up in times of crisis.

"That was a commendable act, young man, but you may be in for trouble," the pastor said to John.

"That soldier has the look of a vicious, revengeful devil. Better steer clear of him. It's times like these that bring out the worst and best that are in a man." With fatherly tenderness he said to Rachael, "Remember, my dear, you are a child of the King. He will protect you from evil."

"Yes, Pastor." She looked at John, her exotic eyes making him feel uncomfortable. Her shy look made a red blush creep slowly up John's face.

"We'd better get busy with the food," he said. A warm feeling of contentment enveloped him, causing some of the anger and cold despair to loosen their stranglehold on his heart. A gentle smile tugged at John's lips.

As the Reverend Worchester turned to leave, John put a restraining hand on his arm. "I'd like to apologize for leaving the meeting this morning, sir. I'm not in the habit of doing things like that. I'm just not myself," John finished lamely.

Worchester smiled sadly. "No, none of us feels like himself these days. Nevertheless, I prefer a man who is either hot or cold toward the Lord. I'm praying for you, John."

John ducked his head uneasily. *Why couldn't this man just be a friend without always bringing God into the conversation?*

With eager hands Charity opened the food bag. Her silvery voice reflected disappointment; "Flour, jerky, and dried beans. What does one do with these? Whatever can this be?" She gingerly held a thick white slab with the tips of her fingers.

"That's hog fat. We can put that in the beans

after they soak. This brown flour we'll make into bread." With a meaningful smile at John, Rachael continued, "Since I'm the sister in this family, perhaps I could cook."

"I am pleased to welcome you into our small family," Mrs. Ross said graciously. She waved a helpless hand toward the food. "But how does one cook these bountiful supplies?" she asked.

A crease marred the serenity of Rachael's forehead as she looked at John. "I'm afraid you will have to get some wood, plus a kettle, some dishes, a large spoon, and whatever else you can acquire from the wagon master. Perhaps it might be wiser to ask Reverend Worchester—"

"No, I'll get the firewood and utensils. You two stay away from that wagon master. As long as we're in this confounded prison, I'll get the food supplies. I don't even want you to come out of the women's building." John's tone was commanding. Rachael smiled. Evidently she enjoyed taking his orders.

John straightened his shoulders, set his jaw in a determined angle, then walked briskly back to the wagon. Fortunately, the man hadn't left.

"I need firewood, cooking utensils, plates, and spoons," John said evenly.

The scowl over the piggish eyes grew deeper, making the man look like a pugnacious giant. John felt like Jack separated from his beanstalk. "What's your name, puppy?"

"Ross."

"Ross, Ross, hm, war'd I hear that there

64

name?" He scratched the back of his head. "By cracky, you're the chief's son!" The man's tight-lipped smile drawn up menacingly at one end sent cold chills down John's spine.

"No," John answered shortly.

"Oh." Disappointment draped the wagon master's face like a shroud. "Still, it might work," he spoke under his breath. He mulled a large wad of tobacco in his mouth thoughtfully. "You rich, pup?" he whispered confidingly.

"Not now," John spat the answer.

A filthy stream of tobacco juice spurted expertly through large yellowed teeth, splattering on John's moccasin. "Don't get uppity with me, pup! Bet your ole man had plenty." A gleeful look contorted his ugly face. He threw the firewood and utensils down to John, who had to move quickly to avoid being struck.

What devilish plan did the man have in mind? Chills made another eerie trip up and down John's spine.

5

Towering above John was an enormous black bull. Almost human, evil, gray eyes glared threateningly at John's defenseless body. The bull snorted. His front legs pawed violently into the red dirt. John searched frantically for a way of escape. He was in an arena, all sides enclosed by impenetrable walls. He could see the flaring red nostrils and feel the bull's fiery breath scorching his face. The bull was playing with him, charging, then turning aside at the last possible moment. Wild-eyed, John searched for a weapon. The bull thundered toward him. This time John knew the bull would not turn.

Abruptly he awoke. His forehead drenched with sweat. The door stood open, flooding the building with hot light. Even the stark reality of prison was welcome this morning. He had slept late again. His head felt better, but some more of that brew would be welcome. He stretched his sore muscles and yawned. He stepped through the open door just in time to see the stockade doors burst open. Two armed soldiers strode inside.

"John Ross, front and center!" the wagon master roared loudly. John stood frozen with unbelief.

66

Was this another nightmare? The wagon master had spotted John. Magically the crowd had melted, isolating him. He stood alone facing the soldiers.

Standing within ten feet of John, they aimed their rifles at him. The guns looked as big as cannons to John. "Come with us. Don't make no trouble," the smaller soldier ordered.

John's eyes sought his mother in the crowd. She looked like she was going to faint. *Good-bye, Mom. I wish I had time to tell you I love you,* John thought as a hard lump stuck in his throat. Priscilla waved a chubby hand, her rosy mouth parted in a smile.

Like a sleepwalker John moved slowly through the stockade doors. They thudded shut behind him. He felt queasy, with a hard knot of fear twisting his stomach. His hands, clenched at his sides, were ice cold and clammy.

"Git over to them trees there on your left," ordered the bull-like wagon master, a tone of triumph lifting his rough voice to a higher pitch.

They marched past the tents of the bivouac army. Off-duty soldiers gave them curious glances as they passed. They strode into the dense woods, far out of earshot of camp.

Is this the end then? Will they shoot me like they did Father? How will it feel to die? Is there really life after death—or nothingness? The uncertainty of what lay ahead—the body so obviously lifeless—where had the life gone? His thoughts were disconnected, whirling madly in his head.

He heard the sadistic chuckling; the soldiers were enjoying their grisly task.

God, give me some more time. I won't fight You anymore. John was surprised to find himself praying.

"That tree there," the wagon master said, pointing to a small tree with a large bullwhip leaning against it. The surge of relief made John's knees weak. *They're not going to shoot me.* The chill fear returned. *Don't let them beat me to death!* he prayed silently.

"Take your shirt off, Ross." The voice held a strange note of endearment, a caressing undertone. With trembling hands, John pulled the buckskin over his head. The smaller soldier picked up a coil of rope lying beside the bullwhip as the big man shoved John roughly against the tree. Two high branches jutted out from each side. Humming a monotonous tune beneath his breath, the wagon master tied John's wrists tightly to the branches. The cruel gray eyes glistened with anticipation. A trickle of tobacco juice rolled unnoticed down the side of his thick lips.

"Where's the gold mine, boy?"

"Gold mine! What are you talking about?"

"Your ole man's gold mine, of course. We got orders to find all the gold mines you Injins stole from us Georgians. Where is it?" The smirk on the broad face revealed the owner was quite certain there was no gold mine.

John's face was white, tight with strain. *O God, don't let them kill me,* he prayed. "There's no gold

68

mine. The only gold around here is in the cornfield. You just found an excuse to whip me because of the girl." John barely recognized the scratchy voice as his own.

The wagon master's leer was plastered tight to his face. "No, boy, you got me all wrong," he said soothingly. "My orders are to find those gold mines. Right, Elkanah? Just tell me where the mine is, and we let you go."

"You might as well tell us. We'll beat it out of you anyway," Elkanah agreed.

When John did not reply, the massive man stepped back, unfurled the bullwhip, and then snapped it viciously in the air. It cracked like a pistol shot, the sound shattering John's nerves. With tightly clenched teeth, he braced himself. Cold sweat stood on his forehead.

Another sharp crack and the whip lashed into his bare back. John's face twisted in pain as the blow shook his whole body. This was worse than anything he had imagined. The whip cut into his flesh, lacerating it to the bone. The second lash made his legs feel like rubber. They wavered, not wanting to hold his weight.

"Where's the gold, you shitepoke?" taunted the wagon master.

With the fourth lash, the agonizing pain radiated to every part of John's body and a red haze filmed his eyes. A scream was stuck in his throat. Then he lost count of the lashes. He hung by his wrists, his legs no longer supporting him. He could not remember when there was no pain. It was a living, breathing monster clawing at his body.

Darkness was in front of his eyes. From far away he heard someone moaning. Then he recognized that it was himself. *Jesus was a better Man than I,* he thought as words Worchester had spoken floated through his mind: "He was oppressed and he was afflicted, yet he opened not his mouth." Then John's brain began to refuse thought. Finally, the merciful darkness came.

Something soft was beneath his head. Was he a small boy cradled in his mother's arms? No, it was a blanket. He was lying face down on the hard ground. He opened his eyes. Back inside the stockade. At first he had no sensation but numbness, then the pain hit. He clutched at the earth, his body shuddering with the intensity.

"Water," he begged. The weakness of his barely audible voice depressed him. His mother brought him some of the tepid water from yesterday's pail. He drank, then turned his face toward the building, closing his eyes. The silent suffering furrowing his face made it evident to the people surrounding him that he wanted to be left alone.

Rachael knelt at his side. "John, I've made a poultice to help ease your pain," she said. "I gathered some healing herbs during the morning worship after they carried you back here. It will sting for a while when I put it on." Gently she laid the dripping poultice on John's back. His body went rigid, then slowly it began to relax as the anesthesia penetrated his lacerated back. He fell into an exhausted sleep.

The next few days were a nightmare of pain, with Rachael, his mother, and the pastor taking turns nursing him. The morning of the fourth day, Rachael was at his side when he opened his eyes, this time with a gourd of medicinal herb tea. John felt weak, but he forced his rubbery arms to prop himself into a position where he could drink the bitter liquid. When the edge of pain softened into a throbbing burn, Rachael asked, "Now that you are feeling better, we can talk. This is the prescribed way of the medicine man. Perhaps you can explain the reason we are being held prisoners."

John looked into Rachael's eyes which were warm with sympathy and sorrow for his suffering. There was no excitement nor joy in her face now. She showed tender concern, a desire to help alleviate his pain. Half-heartedly he began to answer, for talking was not what he felt like doing.

"The worst of our troubles began back in 1802 when the American President Jefferson signed the Georgia Compact. That dastardly compact stated that the United States would give to Georgia all the land owned by our people if Georgia would give all its land to the United States."

"But the Americans had no right to sign that! We owned the land, not they!" Rachael's eyes were wide with indignation.

"That's right. They planned to force us into giving up our land. One way or another, the white

71

man did get control of thousands of acres. Then Uncle John laid down the law. No Indian could sell or give so much as a single section of land to the whites under any circumstances.''

"Yes, I know about that. Mother and Father Brown, the missionaries who took me in when my mother died, thought that Chief Ross was a mighty man of wisdom to make that law. They hated to see the white settlers encroaching more and more on the Cherokee land almost as much as we did.''

"That would have stopped the infernal land grabbing if it hadn't been for Sharp Knife Jackson. Using underhanded methods, he finally succeeded in getting a small faction group to sign a removal treaty three years ago,'' John said bitterly. "The leaders of that group paid with their lives for their treason.''

"Yes, I know. Wasn't that a little severe?'' Her gentle face showed compassion for the three Indians who had been executed Indian fashion for their treason.

"Severe! My father's dead because of those men! We're here in this—'' John clamped his lips shut, not wanting to offend a lady's ears.

Rachael lowered her long lashes, looking at the ground near John's bare shoulder. "But don't you think they were doing what they thought was right?''

"They were guilty of treason, so they paid the penalty. Unfortunately, every Cherokee man, woman, and child will also have to pay severely for what those men accomplished. The treaty was ratified even though the American Secretary of War stated, 'It's no treaty at all, because it is not sanctioned by the great body of the Cherokees.' My father was in the room when he said it.''

''Your father spent a lot of time in Washington, didn't he?''

John enjoyed the admiration her look conveyed. ''Yes. He was Uncle John's spokesman many times. He thought Washington a dreary place for the site of the Americans' government with its muddy streets, few sidewalks, and bad weather. He was always glad to get back to Georgia. Still, I wanted to accompany him, but he needed me to oversee our plantation in his absence. I spent the last two years practically running the plantation single-handedly.'' He grinned when she looked impressed.

He sobered instantly when she asked, ''But why are we being treated this way when all the Americans have is an invalid treaty?''

''It was valid enough for Jackson. He gave us three years to move to Oklahoma Territory. Our laws were declared null and void. On our own land there was no law but the Georgian law. We were permitted no voice in any court of law, so the whites flooded our property, staked claims on our land, and stole any livestock they could get their hands on. Those who defended themselves were put in prison.'' Rachael nodded. She had seen many neighbors hauled to prison, never to return. Only those who were married to white people had any recourse to courts of law, through their spouses.

"Jackson," John spat the name, "contended that the treaty was for our own good because he was giving us more land west of the Mississippi than we owned here. Of course, the Osage Indians already own that land, but that's a minor point with Jackson.

"Land west of the great waters. The region away from the rising sun, called the land of death."

John was silent until Rachael questioned, "How is it that the soldiers caught us by surprise?"

"Uncle John is in Washington right now with a petition signed by 15,665 Cherokee that protests the removal treaty. He still believes in democracy, but his only weapon of defense is public opinion. The American people as a whole are sympathetic toward us. It's only men like Jackson, Governor Gilmer, and a few die-hard frontiersmen who want us expelled. We just didn't think it would ever happen."

"But why did Gilmer and Jackson want to get rid of us?"

"Jackson's an old frontiersman. He remembers the massacres thirty or forty years ago when we were defending our land against the white invaders. Gilmer and the Georgians are just plain hungry—land hungry and gold hungry." John squirmed uncomfortably as his back pain began to sharpen again. "Uncle John advised us to wait patiently for them to find that there was no gold and then they would leave. Instead, they began to steal food and livestock. Uncle John's strategy was to let the white men take and take and take, because he thought that in the end they would become embarrassed by their treatment of us and would leave us in peace on our land. Instead, they held a lottery and gave our land away. Forty acres went to each white man wanting to mine gold and one hundred acres plus sixty was given to any white man who wanted to farm. My father's 700 acres went to a Georgian sergeant. He made some kind of deal with Gilmer to get it all, including our house, but Dad wouldn't give it up without a fight.''

Rachael asked, ''Would it not have been better to leave without resistance? To just go to the new land willingly?''

John didn't reply. He didn't know the answer. He lay back down, wishing for more herbal tea.

Rachael's voice held a sob as she whispered huskily, ''Mother and Father Brown came yesterday.'' John looked up quickly, in time to see her wiping away tears she didn't want him to see. ''I talked with them at the gate,'' she continued. ''They begged General Scott to let them take me home. Mother Brown promised they would adopt me legally, but General Scott refused. He said they were too old, they're both in their sixties. It broke my heart, John, to see them so unhappy.'' Rachael cleared her throat and paused for a moment before going on. ''They brought me some fruit,'' she then said in a calmer tone. ''I saved this peach for you.''

John bit into the ripe fruit with pleasure. Never could he remember anything tasting so good. He was not surprised that the general had denied the missionaries' request, but he knew that voicing his anger would not help Rachael.

"Tsiwanihu tocu [I speak the truth], you not look good," a young baritone voice said suddenly.

Craning his head to look up at the speaker, John saw a tall, dark Indian youth with a muscular, well-knit body standing close to Rachael. His shining, black eyes revealed a zest for living plus high intelligence.

Rachael welcomed the newcomer warmly. "John, I'd like you to meet Bold Hunter. Bold Hunter, this is John Ross."

John felt annoyed. The young man was easily the best-looking Indian he had ever seen. He was tall and strong, with a look of fearless freedom about him. Obviously he was a full-blooded Cherokee. *Why did he have to make an appearance now while I'm flat on my chest?* John thought. *Where did he come from anyway? I haven't seen him before.* No new group of captives had been brought in since John's capture.

John was in too much pain now to solve that riddle. The numbness the tea had provided was wearing off. The heat sizzled up from the ground. He felt like a piece of bacon frying on a griddle. The mounting pressure from the pain in his back caused him to writhe on his blanket.

"Excuse me, I must make another poultice," Rachael murmured, going swiftly to her task.

76

The young Indian spoke with contempt, "Cherokee never show pain. You not much Cherokee!" He turned and glided swiftly after Rachael.

6

John measured the next several days in segments of painful minutes slowly ticking into hours. Bold Hunter became a daily but unwelcome visitor. At first, John had tried to be friendly.

"Thanks for helping Rachael make the poultices and herbal tea," he had said as cheerfully as he could manage. Bold Hunter had not answered.

"I'm obliged to you for picking up the noon provisions," John went on. "Your added food and water give each of us a little more to live on." Bold Hunter still looked at John coldly, his face impassive.

John smiled, trying his best to be sincere. "We might as well be friends—" The look of disdain from the Indian's hard black eyes stopped him in mid-sentence. John felt the anger in him boil up. A few days earlier he would have made good his reputation as a hotspur, but now he was weak as a newborn kitten. *When I get on my feet, that arrogant full blood is going to become a former member of this family.* John thought darkly.

Rachael ignored the stony silence between the two young men. As John required less constant care, she asked Bold Hunter to build a shelter from the sun for Charity and Priscilla. Their fair skin was burned raw beneath the blistering sun. Using the bark peeled only from the east side of birch trees, Bold Hunter built a temporary shelter. Charity could sit upright beneath its scant protection, sheltered from the sun's rays most of the day.

Priscilla became an unending source of delight as John lay watching her through the long days. He began to realize she was a real little person, not just the baby Mother was always occupied with.

Under Rachael's direction, Bold Hunter moved their campfire near the two shelters. Rachael laughingly dubbed it the "summer kitchen," referring to the small houses built outside large plantation homes where the food was prepared during the hot summer months.

Today John watched with eager eyes as Rachael kindled a fire on the smooth rocks. Then she swept the hard-packed red clay dirt clean of embers; when she finished, she laid a loaf of wheat dough on the dirt. Next she covered it with a deep clay dish. Building up the fire, she baked the bread.

The delicious aroma of the baking bread made John's empty stomach cramp. Her face rosy from the heat of the fire, Rachael carefully lifted the dish. The bread was browned to perfection. When it had cooled, the tasty bread didn't last long.

Later, when the stockade emptied for the morning worship, John pushed himself up into a sitting position. His back felt stiff and unnatural, but the pain had subsided to a continual dull throbbing burn. Moving his back as little as possible, he got shakily to his feet. Leaning against the men's building for support, he willed his legs to hold him upright. Walking stiffly like a wooden soldier, his right arm braced against the side of the building, John wobbled the length of the building, then back to his bed. It felt gratifying to be on his feet again. *My muscles got so weak from lack of use,* he thought. *But my back doesn't feel any worse while I'm standing up than it did while I was lying down. Can't take much of that sun. Wonder where my shirt is?*

Feeling depressed over his weakness, the solitude of the hot, empty prison, and his stomach which was still signaling its need for food, John gingerly settled himself back on his blanket. He laid his head heavily on his folded arms, closing his eyes against the brilliant sunlight.

He heard footsteps. His low spirits rose when he saw Rachael approaching. She looked fresh, vigorous, and unbelievably lovely.

"John," she said softly, sitting down close to his side, "do you believe a man is bound to keep a promise?"

John raised his eyebrows and smiled a quizzical half smile. "Any man of integrity will keep his word. A promise is not made lightly." He wondered what could be so important to keep her away from Worchester's sermon.

Rachael sat looking at him. He couldn't read the expression in her eyes, but he felt that what she wanted to say was very important to her. As he sat

80

up in order to face her, the sting of pain in his back reminded him to move more slowly.

"After they carried you back in here," she began, not looking at him, "they just threw you down in the dirt. Everyone got busy finding a blanket for you, getting what medicine we could and so on. I—I was afraid you were dying. You lay there so white and limp, with blood dripping all over you. I begged God to let you live. I promised Him that if He did that I would try very hard to help you become a Christian."

John felt his cheeks burn. So that's why she had come. The depressed feeling returned. She was more interested in his soul than in him.

"Then, when I was trying to wash the blood off," Rachael continued, "just before you regained consciousness, you began moaning and muttering."

John thought with a desperate sinking in his stomach, *What on earth did she hear me say when I was out cold?* He stared intently at the ground, a flush red tinging his lean cheeks. Slapping gently at the ever-present pesky flies that continually alighted on his exposed back, he finally muttered, "What did I say?"

"You said, 'If they don't kill me, I'll stop fighting you.' I think you were talking to God." Rachael answered his barely audible question brightly, as though the words felt good in her mouth. She talked so easily about God that John began to feel less self-conscious. He hoped that was all he had said.

"Yes, you're right, and I mean to keep my word," he admitted. "It's just that I don't know how." John forced the words out, for he didn't like to admit his ignorance.

Rachael's gaze was concentrated on the open stockade door, but John sensed that she was seeing something far beyond the door—something he could not see.

"Have you ever been lonely?" Her voice held a faraway note.

"Yes, I was lonely before you came."

"No, I mean *really* lonely—so lonely that you felt you were an empty skin, a broken bowl. That once you were filled with warmth and love but it all seeped out through the break in your life. No matter how hard you tried you couldn't regain the security and comfort you had lost. Your life was empty."

"I felt a little like that when I lost Dad. But I think I feel more bitter than empty."

Rachael's eyes lost their faraway expression. "A bowl of bitter water is fit only to be tossed onto the dust. The bitter waters can be turned sweet just as loneliness can become love."

John shrugged slightly. Rachael saw the disbelief in his eyes, but she decided to continue. "I never knew my father. He died before I was born. My mother was beautiful. Many braves competed for her moccasins to rest inside their cabin, but she refused them all. She said that the great spirit had punished her for her sin by taking my father before they could be married."

John tried to hide his shock.

"My mother loved me. I was happy until she died. No family in the clan would take me in because my mother's people refused to give me their name. I was only twelve, but even then young men wanted me. But I was not willing to marry; I was afraid." Rachael looked steadily at her hands as she continued to speak with an effort.

John was totally caught up in her story. He could picture the beautiful child, alone in the world, her past making her an outsider, her beauty prodding the young braves into approaching her, and her fear binding her.

"One young man was very kind. He hunted game for me. But when he brought the wild turkey, I could not eat. His attention only made me weep. At length he persuaded me to go with him to the home of the white missionary many miles away, even though he was not a Christian. The missionaries were very kind; they insisted that I live with them. I stayed because I did not care what became of me. Then Mother and Father Brown told me that the Lord Jesus wanted to come into my life and fill me with His love. I decided if this was not true, I would kill myself." She looked at John then, tears reddening her eyes. "I made my decision. I no longer wished to live. If God was real, He would have to prove it to me. If not, I had some hemlock in a small pouch tied around my neck."

John gasped. Had she really been so desperate? He could not conceive anyone taking his own life.

83

But they were of different temperaments. At times he had glimpsed a brooding personality beneath her loving, helpful nature.

"I went upstairs into the beautiful bedroom Mother Brown had prepared for me. I set the candle on the little table next to the window and slipped onto my knees beside the window seat. That was my favorite nook in all the world. From there I could see across the orchard to the little white church where Father Brown preached. It was early spring. I remember the apple blossoms. I don't think I've ever seen so many before or since that year." The way she related her story, John could almost smell the apple blossoms.

"I was crying because I could not respond to the love which Mother and Father were giving to me. I was afraid I would never be able to love anyone again. Then I closed my eyes and asked, 'Jesus, will You come into my heart?'"

After a few seconds of silence had elapsed, John asked, "What happened?"

"It's difficult for me to tell. I had a precious experience and I don't want you to ridicule it or laugh. The only reason I'm telling you this is because I made a promise to God." She looked almost angry.

"But from that time on you were able to love?" John's voice was gentle.

"Not only love, but oh, ever so much more! Life is a beautiful gift. Eternal life enables us to enjoy it."

John didn't want to ask, but his mental integrity forced him. "Isn't it a little too easy?"

Rachael's eyes were wide, her face soft and tender, her usually mysterious smile replaced by a smile of such love and tenderness that John's heart began to race. "Yes, it's easy for us because Jesus paid the price. He died in our place and took the punishment for our shortcomings." Impulsively, she took his hand. "It's just like what you did; because you protected me from the wagon master, you suffered instead of me. You took my place. I think that even if you had known that the wagon master was going to bullwhip you that you still would have protected me!"

John was not so certain. He was glad he hadn't known the cost. For an instant the suffocating fear he had experienced when he thought the wagon master was going to kill him flashed through his mind.

"So you see, becoming a child of God is a gift," Rachael continued. "All you need to do is accept the gift. The Giver paid for it and offers it freely to you. Will you take it?" Her eyes earnestly pleaded as she sat leaning toward him, waiting for his answer.

"I need to think about it. I'll let you know what I decide."

Some of the joy faded from Rachael's face, but she smiled as she said, "Whatever you say."

A sound like wind gently rustling dry leaves made them both look up. The prisoners were returning. Men trudged in, shoulders hunched, faces

85

tired with defeat. The women were enduring their imprisonment with quiet fortitude. Only the small children seemed unaffected. They joined together in various games or clung to an older brother or sister in hope of a story. Yet, many of the faces burned with a look of strength John could not fathom.

Mother walked slowly across the compound toward them. She looked out of place in the rude prison. Rachael must have combed her thick blonde hair into that graceful spiral on top of her head. Her delicate green dress, now stained with perspiration, had been exactly right in her airy drawing room; but here it exposed her pale shoulders and neck to the pitiless sun. She had always been so careful to protect her skin from sunburn. Her green, high-heeled slippers were too thin for walking on the rough ground. John swallowed hard as he looked at her. How was he going to be able to take care of her?

"Your suffering has hurt her deeply" Rachael said sadly, reading his thoughts. "She is so proud of your courage, but she hates the price you had to pay. Courage always costs; sometimes it costs a lot."

"Yes, but it's harder to live with yourself if you're a coward. Um, did you tell Mother what you told me? About Christ, I mean?"

"Yes, that first night in the stockade. She was terribly depressed because your father had been killed. I told her that God cares for her no matter what man may do. She accepted God's gift of eternal life. I don't think she would have had the strength to face life any longer without God's help. She's not very strong."

John grunted. He felt glad his mother had Someone to lean on, but he still wasn't sure he needed that.

"Your mother's been making a shirt for you from one of her petticoats," Rachael said. "It looks like she has it finished. You should be up and walking now to get your strength back." John was happy to see the shirt folded over his mother's arm. "I thought Bold Hunter would offer you his shirt since he's just about your size, but he didn't." Rachael seemed puzzled at the young Indian's lack of helpfulness.

John was pleased that Bold Hunter hadn't offered. The thought of owing him a favor wasn't exactly a happy one.

7

The day began exactly as each tedious scorching day had during the two and a half months since the wagon master had taken his revenge on John. He had no premonition that today was going to be different.

The sun was slowly boiling the people being held captive inside the stockade. During the early days of imprisonment when townspeople from what had been New Echota passed outside the stockade, they had heard the sounds of masses of people living inside. Recently, however, no sound came from within the walls—no babble of voices, no crying of children—all was a puzzling silence.

Along with most of the other captives, John had recently been suffering dysentery. He figured the cramping diarrhea which sapped his strength must have come from the water rations. Flies swarmed within the enclosure in the daylight hours; mosquitoes plagued the captives during the night. Between the diarrhea and the sun, John felt as if every ounce of fluid in his body had dried up. Even though the days continued blazing hot and humid, he perspired very little. A languor settled over him like a blanket that he wished he could throw off.

The silence jangled John's nerves. The only relief of the day came when the big doors swung open for the worship service. Listening to Worchester beneath the relative cool of the trees was the big event of each day. Back at Pleasant Acres, John wouldn't have bothered attending such a service, but now it was his only escape from boredom, the almost unbearable heat, the stench of human waste, and a nagging restlessness.

From where he sat cross-legged in the dirt, he could see most of the people as they sat or lay motionless on the bone-dry red earth. The merciless heat drained all energy from the body. No one talked. Families sat together, drawing comfort from the nearness of their loved ones. Many sat with closed eyes, receiving comfort in prayer. John felt he had kept his promise to God; he wasn't fighting Him anymore, not that he had any excess strength to use. No, he wasn't fighting, but he didn't feel drawn to God either. Still, he had plenty of time to think about the things Rachael had told him.

The doors opened. Listlessly the people rose to their feet, shuffling out to the relative freedom beneath the trees. *There must be at least a thousand of us jammed in here,* John thought. *Wonder when we'll go to Oklahoma? Anything will be better than this.*

John carried Priscilla, and Charity took her son's arm. She was barefoot now, having long since worn out her slippers. Walking beside Charity was Rachael, Bold Hunter sticking closer to her than a burr.

Of late the soldiers had permitted the people to bathe in the cool stream running through the meadow. John licked his dry lips in anticipation of the short dip. Worchester had insisted that the women bathe at one end, with the men and boys at the other. Most of the guard was concentrated at the women's end.

Today John took Pris in, for his mother looked exceptionally tired. Pris quickly threw off her lethargy while John played with her in the cool water. Her tiny body was so fragile. *Such a faint hold a child has on life,* John thought. She paddled her tiny hands in the water. When she splashed John, he made a funny face and she giggled and laughed. Her tinkling laugh made him feel so good that he performed various antics for her benefit.

Seated on the ground after their dip, the people felt revived and listened intently to Pastor Worchester. Pris curled in her mother's arms for a nap, and John stretched out full length on the soft grass and moss beneath the trees. If it had not been for this free time each day, he was sure that he and all the other Indians would have gone insane. Such a luxury to lie in the shade without someone's elbow in your back! He had to admit that Worchester was pretty interesting too.

"Difficulty is a severe teacher," the pastor said. "When the wind blows on a tree, the roots stretch and get stronger. So it is with us. When the winds of adversity blow, we shall stretch spiritually and

90

become strong. We shall not go into exile as weaklings. 'Hast thou not heard, that the everlasting God, the LORD, the Creator . . . fainteth not, neither is weary? . . . He giveth power to the faint; and to them that have no might he increaseth strength. Even the youths shall faint and be weary, and the young men shall utterly fall: but they that wait upon the LORD shall renew their strength; they shall mount up with wings as eagles; they shall run, and not be weary; and they shall walk, and not faint.'"*

Worchester's voice rumbled on, but John didn't hear it. The words, "To them that have no might he increaseth strength . . . they shall walk, and not faint," echoed so loud in John's mind that he couldn't hear anything else. He had never regained his original strength after being whipped. Day by day the lack of good food plus the dysentery and the scorching sun were draining his remaining strength. So little exercise and the aimless life had also taken their toll.

What kind of strength is Worchester talking about? he wondered. *Is it physical or mental or spiritual? Maybe all three? Whatever it is, I need it!*

He lay on his tender back looking up into a leafy tree. Sunlight slashed its way through the shade here and there where the leaves were not thick enough to screen it out. An inchworm humped its way across the lowest limb. Before it had gone

*Isaiah 40:28-31

halfway to its destination, John had made a decision. *It worked for Rachael; maybe it will work for me.* He flipped over onto his stomach, buried his face in his hands, and closed his eyes. The earthly smell of moist ground and moss filled his nostrils. "O God," he prayed silently, "if You've got this strength for me, I accept it." Slowly a deep peace settled over him as an unseen Presence entered his life. A feeling of strength and joy flowed throughout his innermost self. His amazed reaction was *This is real!* Opening his eyes, he looked at a new world. He was born again.

Later, when the people got up to return to the stockade, John began to whistle. It wasn't easy to whistle with dry, cracked lips, but the joy inside had to come out. Seeing Rachael staring at him, he grinned. A smile began on her lips until it lighted her whole face.

John felt the invisible barrier between them dissolve. Bold Hunter's eyes knifed him between the shoulders, but he didn't care. John's strong hand closed gently around hers.

The next day after worship service, he stood in the stream again. Today, he was the only one being baptized. Armed soldiers stood along one edge of the bank, no longer curious or even insolent, for so many people had been baptized during the past weeks that they had grown indifferent. They stood, guns lying uncocked over their arms. Bold Hunter stood near them, his lips twisted in a sarcastic smile.

John looked at the other bank where his mother,

Rachael, and Pris were standing amid hundreds of believing Christians. Their faces were full of quiet serenity which almost covered the lines of hunger and weariness. John could feel the cold indifference on one side, the tenderness and love on the other. He wondered why he had waited so long to change sides.

The birds sang high in the trees arching over the banks of the river. John could pick out the trill of the meadowlark. Looking beyond the people to the rolling hills, he saw a purple haze hanging low, almost sliding into the valleys. The fields were laid out like a patchwork quilt over an uneven bed, the fenced-in farmhouses and yards looking neat and tranquil in the sunlight.

The little pastor splashed toward him from the right bank. John stood in the center of the stream, water swirling about his waist. The pastor began to question him. "Have you received Christ as your Saviour?"

"Yes, sir, I have," John answered, his clear baritone voice ringing firmly.

"John McCormac Ross, I baptize you in the name of the Father, and of the Son, and of the Holy Spirit." The Reverend Worchester deftly gripped John's hands with one of his own, put his other hand on the small of John's back, and then slid him into the water. After Worchester lifted him up, he said, "This baptism signifies your identity with Christ in death, burial, and resurrection. Walk now in newness of life."

John automatically shook his head, sending a

shower of water from his thick blond hair in all directions. Without a backward look at the hostile shore, he splashed over to stand with the other believers. Quite a few of the pretty girls were smiling at him, and the Christian men crowded around to shake his hand. Mother hugged him while Rachael looked as radiant as a bride.

John's step was springy as he walked back to the prison. His tall frame was relaxed, moving with that inner air of superiority that set him apart from other men. Even in his faded buckskin with the makeshift shirt, John Ross still looked as if he owned the world, a prince turned by ill fortune into a pauper. Or *was* it ill fortune?

The blush on Rachael's cheeks did not pale. Her eyes seemed too bright; they were glittering. "Do you feel well?" John asked, concerned.

"No, I began to feel sick just before you were baptized. I thought I was just excited, but now I'm not so sure."

Her hair, falling freely to her waist, was not as glossy as usual, and her normal rosy lips looked pale. She raised a slender hand to her forehead. "I've got a blinding headache."

"Let's get you out of this sun and under the lean-to," John said, putting an arm around her shoulder and hurrying her toward the prison. Abruptly she stopped, turned her back to him, her body heaving. She tried to make it to a nearby tree, but couldn't. She vomited repeatedly. He tried to help her, but she shook him off. "Leave me alone.

94

Go away," she begged between bouts. John stood looking at her helplessly.

In a few minutes Rachael began to shiver. John got her over to to the lean-to, gave her a drink, and ran to get Charity. Mrs. Ross looked closely at the sick girl lying beneath the peeled bark structure and said, "John, don't come near. I'm fairly certain Rachael has smallpox."

A cold chill of fear ran down John's spine. Visions of Rachael's beautiful face marred with pox marks flashed before his eyes. Almost without thinking, he began to pray silently for her.

"What about you, Mother? If you take care of her, you might catch it. Let me take care of her."

"You can't, John. There are some things you just can't do. Besides, I need you to watch Pris. I'm afraid she's already been exposed, but perhaps not." His mother looked searchingly into her baby daughter's face. A look of worry flitted over her features, quickly erased by a look of forced cheerfulness. "Thank God you had smallpox when you were ten," she said to her son.

John cradled Pris in his arms, the innocent blue eyes looking up at him with love and trust. She smiled a tired little smile before her curly lashes dropped closed on her rounded cheek.

He held the sleeping child tenderly. "What am I going to do with you?" he asked softly. Bold Hunter came over.

"You turn into squaw. First you get Christian like old man; now you become squaw." He stood with his arms folded across his broad chest, his lips

95

curled into a contemptuous smile. The way he spoke, the words became flaming symbols of scorn.

John felt a flush start at the base of his neck, then spread to his face until he was burning. He stared intently at his frayed moccasins. Biting his lip, he held back the angry retort that came so quickly to mind. He was a Christian now. What would a Christian do? He didn't know. All he knew was that he wanted to smash his fist into that leering face. The taste of hate was bitter on his tongue.

The sudden tension in his body woke Priscilla and she started to cry in fright. John wanted to put her down; then he'd show Bold Hunter who was a squaw.

"You not even good squaw," Bold Hunter taunted as Pris's crying grew louder when her mother did not appear. That was too much. John slid the crying child to the ground and in one smooth movement was facing Bold Hunter, knees bent, hands half extended. John knew he was fast. They were both the same height, but Bold Hunter outweighed him by about twenty-five pounds. He looked tough, but John figured he could take him. Dad had made sure he was trained to take care of himself.

"What's wrong with the little girl?" Sam Worchester's voice boomed between the two young men, effectively halting them. "Looks like she's been scared. Here, little miss. Big brother is right here. He will take care of you." Sam lifted the baby up, putting her into John's arms. Worchester ignored the pending fight.

John fought his anger. The effort caused his hands to tremble so much that he almost dropped Priscilla. Bold Hunter's look said he thought John was scared.

"John, Christ in you means His love is in you," the pastor said. "Hate destroys. It's easy to hate an enemy. Christ wants you to love your enemies and pray for them. It takes a Christian to do that." Then he turned to Bold Hunter with a warm smile, "Son, I've been praying for you," he said. "I'm available if you ever want to talk with me alone."

Bold Hunter snorted rudely and spat. "I no need squaw power. I got big medicine power—power from shaman to make woman love me." He looked defiantly at Worchester and John, obviously preferring the ancient methods of the witch doctor to the new Christianity of the white man.

Pris stopped crying. Worchester offered John a piece of blanket to make a sling over one shoulder for carrying her. She wrapped her thin legs around John, clinging to him while asking for her mother.

"Is there any way we can get milk for Pris?" John asked, ignoring Bold Hunter. "She's lost so much weight that I'm really worried about her."

"My daughter, Hope, just got into town yesterday from the East," the pastor replied. "She's bringing milk here tomorrow for the young children. I'm to meet her at noon when the gate opens for the wagon master. We'll be certain that Pris gets some every day while Hope is here. The mili-

97

tary says we'll be moving out in September, and that's just a couple more weeks."

John's spirits soared with the thought of activity. Anything was better than rotting in this stinking stockade. The thought of being free again was keenly tantalizing.

Having decided that the two young men were cooled off sufficiently and that it was safe to leave them alone, Worchester said in parting, "Meet me at the gate tomorrow. I'll introduce you to my daughter, John."

After the pastor left, John turned to face Bold Hunter to see if he still wanted to fight. John was more than willing, but surprisingly, Bold Hunter said, "We talk."

The sun blazed overhead. John settled Pris comfortably in her sling bed, shielding her from the hot rays with his own shadow.

"Bold Hunter not captured by soldiers. Come here alone," the Indian stated flatly.

"Why?" John looked into the fierce black eyes challenging his own.

"Bold Hunter live near Rachael in mountains. Know her since young boy. Take her to live with white missionaries when she alone. She my woman. Before Bold Hunter come inside, meet Rachael outside stockade under trees while short man preaches. Tell Rachael come, escape to mountains, hide in caves. No soldiers find us there. She no come. She say she must help white baby and momma." Bold Hunter glared at the sleeping Pris. "Me know how to get her away. Rachael no come. She needed here she say."

John was so surprised he could only stare dumbly at Bold Hunter.

"If Rachael die, Bold Hunter kill John Ross!"

8

Bold Hunter lifted his fringed deerskin shirt. Strapped around his muscular chest was a thin rawhide strap which cleverly fastened a short hunting knife into a concealed position beneath his left arm where the soldiers were unlikely to search.

The naked hate in the young Indian's eyes made John's back stiffen. Love your enemies and pray for them? He would have to pray with his eyes open! He stood glaring back into Bold Hunter's eyes, a small part of his mind questioning *how* to love his enemies. Curious faces were looking at them, perhaps hoping to see a fight. With the tensions and irritabilities brought on by hunger and heat, tempers had flared often within the stockade, resulting in numerous fights.

The electric tension seemed to spread in ever-widening circles around them until John felt that surely the whole stockade full of prisoners would form a circle about them, urging them to settle their difference immediately.

Suddenly Bold Hunter grunted, turned on his heel, then stalked away. John wiped the sweat off his forehead with the back of a shaking hand. "Women!" he muttered. "I am stuck with three of them. Sure wish Dad were here. At least he could have taken care of two of them. Maybe he took the easy way out."

John wasn't scared of Bold Hunter. He just didn't want to make any mistakes in this new Christian way of life. *What makes a Christian different from other people?* he wondered. *I know full well how I'm different on the inside. But does a Christian fight? Well, God is living inside me now. He'll just have to teach me what He wants me to know.* The quiet peace of living in unity with God settled over him, calming his tightened nerves. He began to whistle. Several tired, hot faces looked his way again in surprise. They began to smile.

At noon the next day John stood in front of the wagon master waiting for his rations. "What do we have here? A pretty new squaw in camp!" The wagon master spoke with an insinuating tone that made John's anger flame as he waited with Priscilla snug in her sling under his arm.

Facing the cruel wagon master each noon was always torture, for the beefy man got some morbid kind of satisfaction from humiliating him. John always attempted to remain cool, ignoring the man's taunts, while unconsciously spurring the man on with his innate attitude of superiority.

"Ain't this a nasty place for such a nice young squaw? You don't look very strong, Miss. Maybe somebody ought to take care of you 'stead of you

101

takin' care of that papoose." The man's heavy jowls creased into an unpleasant snarl. His lips pulled back over his large yellow teeth, as he shot a stream of tobacco juice expertly. John side-stepped. With a calmness he didn't feel, he looked up into the cold gray eyes, almost colorless but for the dark slate in their deepest recesses. "I'm waiting for my supplies," John said evenly.

"Tarnation! You can wait until I'm good and ready to give them to you, squaw. I serve men first. Just mebby there won't be nothin' left when I get done. Don't you come over here tellin' me what to do like some big shot, when you ain't nothin' but a dirty half-breed injin." His broad face was contorted with hate.

John clenched his fists at his side. Beneath the high, slightly protruding forehead, narrowed blue eyes burned with a hatred he knew he shouldn't be feeling. *How much of this can a man endure and keep his self-respect? Love your enemies and pray for them? Even when they have me helpless and squirming, Lord?* he asked silently. His temples throbbing, John slowly unclenched his fists. His taut face relaxed. He stood in the blazing sun, waiting.

Working with slow deliberation, the wagon master handed out the supplies to the long line of Indians. The sympathetic looks coming his way didn't make John feel any better. *Pris will be waking soon,* he thought, *and she'll be hungry. I've got to hurry and get the fire started and get something cooking for her.* As he looked down at the sleeping face half buried against his chest, his face burned hot with helpless rage.

Twenty more minutes and the man was finally done. John stepped in front of the wagon as the man picked up the oxen reins to leave.

"Hold on!" he yelled desperately. "Give me my rations."

"Ask me nice" came the insinuating voice from the wagon bed.

John's self-restraint snapped. They *had* to have that food and water! The skimpy two meals a day they got from the rations weren't even enough. They were always enduring the painful gnawing ache that continued hunger produces. And now Rachael needed extra water because of her fever.

Swiftly placing Pris on the ground, John leaped aboard the wagon bed and grabbed two bags full of rations from the dirty floor. His voice gritty with rage, he said through clenched teeth, "Now give me my water—I need extra because of sickness—or so help me, I'll see that you get what's coming to you!"

With amazing speed for such a heavy man, the wagon master's foot shot out, kicking John squarely in the chest with his thick boot and knocking him backward out of the wagon. With a painful "whooosh," the breath left John's lungs as he landed flat on his back on the rock-hard red clay. The man's booming laughter rang harshly in the hot still air. "You whelp! I can break you in half anytime I feel like it. But I'd sooner see you sittin' in this here stockade. I like to watch your hide turn brown while you roast. But one of these days I'm gonna get tired of waitin'. Then I'm gonna give you another taste of Ole Bess here." He flicked the bullwhip, and the oxen jerked nervously. "But when I do, I ain't gonna stop till your hide's been cut into ribbons. You understand that, boy?"

Lying on his back while struggling to breathe, John held on to the food sacks tightly with both fists. His face had grown pale beneath his tan, and his lips were white.

"Till then, I'm gonna keep you fattened up. You look as skinny as a starving wolf." With exaggerated helpfulness, the hulking man jumped heavily from the wagon and carried two brimming buckets of water to John. "There, squaw. Don't say big Ben McDonal never done you a favor." His eyes twitched. His face squinted into a cruel smile.

John saw a sinister gleeful look in the man's eyes as he stared down at him. *He's itching to kick me. I wonder what's stopping him,* flashed through his mind. Beside him Priscilla was crying in frightened shrieks. When McDonal finally raised a heavy boot, John curved himself protectively around Pris. But then the big wagon master changed his mind. His slow-moving thoughts were written plainly on his harsh face. Glee was erased by cunning, and the cunning wiped clean by an assumed look of respectful attention. He plodded away.

Slowly John sat up just as two soldiers, their blue uniforms bright with gold braid, rode inside the stockade. An unexpected inspection by some top brass! That's what had stopped McDonal. His breath racking his body with pain, John cuddled Pris, not attempting to talk. Gradually the little girl's choking sobs grew quieter. When John gave her a drink from one of the water pails, she smiled through her tears and settled back against his dirty shirt. John brushed at the big red boot mark on his shirt, only succeeding in making it a muddy white. His face reflected his dark thoughts against the wagon master.

Awkwardly, his progress hampered by the baby, John hauled the food and water to their campsite. A sudden thought made him smack his forehead in dismay. "Worchester's daughter!" He glanced at the stockade door. It was still open. Grabbing a drinking gourd, he rushed with Pris toward the gate.

As he approached it, McDonal was standing near the supply wagon talking with the two officers. John strode quickly past them toward the gate. He certainly didn't feel like meeting anyone, but he had given his word that he would be there.

Still fuming inwardly over his encounter with McDonal, John met the Reverend Worchester and his daughter.

"You got here just in time, John," the pastor said. "They'll be closing the gates soon. We've already given milk to the other young children but have saved enough for Pris. We've been waiting quite a while. What kept you? Hope, this is John Ross. John, my daughter." Worchester's jovial voice rang with pride.

Trying to erase the frown from his face, John unconsciously rubbed a dirty hand across his forehead. His effort left a reddish brown streak. All he could think about was that he had to hurry because Pris was hungry. And that bully McDonal! Someday he would—

The dimpled smile faded from Hope Worchester's face as she looked up into John's frowning, obviously impatient, gaze. The warm lights in her wide green eyes flickered out, leaving them as cool and distant as white-capped mountains. John felt a sinking sensation in the pit of his stomach.

He suddenly became conscious of how he must look. Dirty shirt, threadbare britches, moccasins with holes so large that his toes protruded, and long blond hair, uncut for months. Suddenly he was embarrassed carrying Priscilla. His smile was stiff and forced. "I'm pleased to meet you, Miss Worchester," he said woodenly.

She was small, the top of her coal-scuttle bonnet barely reaching his shoulder. And she was so clean and well dressed that she seemed to be from a different planet. He was too accustomed to seeing the tattered people inside the stockade. The lacy mitts protecting her hands from the sun didn't belong in his stark world.

Hope Worchester wasn't beautiful, but vibrancy radiated around her like a halo. If she and Rachael ever stood together, most eyes would be dazzled by Hope before noticing the more quiet beauty of Rachael. After that, a matter of personal preference would determine the gaze.

Shifting his weight uneasily from one foot to the other, John tossed his hair back from his eyes with a jerk. For such a tiny person, she could really make him feel uncomfortable. He knew he should say something. But he just stood there, drinking in the healthy, free, neat freshness of her. How many worlds ago had he been on the outside? He knew his fixed stare was beginning to embarrass the girl, but he was powerless.

John saw character, courage, and much determination in the strong round chin and steady gaze that returned his so coolly. Warmth of passion showed in the curve of her lips. "Your most humble servant, ma'am," he said tautly, and then flushed as he realized that he had already acknowledged her.

If Pastor Worchester hadn't come to his rescue, she would have let him stand there mumbling like a fool all day. "This is Priscilla, John's baby sister. He's caring for her while Mrs. Ross nurses those who are ill with smallpox."

Hope reached eagerly for Priscilla, her face delightful in its young maternal look. But the pastor quickly stepped between Hope and the baby. "No, my dear," he apologized. "I'm afraid that the baby may have been exposed to smallpox. I'm sorry, but I must ask you not to touch her," he finished gently.

Hope stepped back, her face hidden in the shadow of her sunbonnet. Then she turned to fill a gourd with the remainder of the milk she had brought. "Give this to the sweet little girl, please,

107

Daddy," she asked with a slight tremble in her voice. Obligingly, the pastor poured the milk into the gourd John held. Replacing the milk gourd on its hook on the bucket, Hope half turned from the men, but not before John noticed a spot glistening on her cheek. When she straightened, it was gone.

"They're closing the gate now. I'll see you tomorrow, dear," the pastor said.

Hope kissed her father. Turning to John, she said coolly, "It was a pleasure to meet you, Mr. Ross." The girl's tone suggested delicately that it definitely had *not* been a pleasure to meet Mr. Ross.

John was furious. The girl could get lost for all he cared! But immediately he realized that he *did* care. The prick to his masculine pride had been painful. Hope Worchester obviously wasn't the sweet, docile, plain preacher's daughter he had expected her to be.

9

Pris greedily drank the milk the Worchester girl had brought. John surmised that the two soldiers lingering near the gate must have carried the milk buckets for Hope. He laughed shortly. *They're trying to look so casual,* he thought, *but eagerness is seeping out of their pores like sweat. They can't wait to walk her back into town!*

Seeing John frowning darkly at the closed stockade doors, Worchester's green eyes crinkled kindly as he peered over the top of rimless glasses. "Losing one's freedom is not easy," he commented. "I'm rather curious to find out what happened to you. You looked as angry as Moses thundering down Mount Sinai the way you came storming over to meet Hope. Your eyes were blazing with blue wrath. I could almost see smoke curling out of your ears. Did you have another encounter with Bold Hunter?"

"No, sir. Ben McDonal, the wagon master, makes me crawl every time I go for the rations. It just got to be more than I could handle today, that's all," John answered gruffly.

"I see." Worchester frowned and looked as if he was about to offer his services as the food-supply man for the Rosses, so John quickly changed the subject.

"You have a fine daughter, sir."

"Yes. I see she took you by surprise. She's been taking people by surprise all her life. She's a strong-minded girl. My parishes expected her to fit into a specified mold. 'Pristine, pure, and pallid,' she called it with disgust. She refused, insisting on being herself in every way. What could I do?" Worchester threw up his hands in resignation. John wondered if this godly man had a thorn in his side.

"What can a man do? I lost my wife when she was born. Should have taken another, but the years swept by and the right one never came along, though goodness knows, many a dear lady had designs." John laughed.

"I sent her off to the strictest finishing school in Boston. But then she wrote and begged me to let her come along on the wagon train to Oklahoma. I hadn't been getting the best of reports on her behavior at school and I missed her terribly, so I decided to let her come. She immediately took matters into her own hands, sold all our household furniture, most of our clothes, and anything else she could get her little hands on. She even held a couple of fund-raising bazaars. Used the money to buy blankets and clothes for the Indians. She talked the government into issuing us a team of oxen and a wagon, and here she is. The milk she finagled out of the army. Yes, between the two of them, I've—well, let's talk about your problem."

110

"You have another daughter, sir?"

"No, a son. Just a bit older than you. He's in the Regular Army. But that's another story. Which gets us back to you. Who's doing your cooking now that Rachael's sick?"

"I am. I watched Rachael enough, so I think I can handle it. Besides, it gives me something to do. I've got strict orders to stay away from Mom and Rachael. After I prepare their food, Mom will come over to pick it up."

"What about you? Have you had smallpox?"

"Yes, sir. When I was ten. Mom's good at nursing; she pulled me through."

"I'm happy to hear that. Rachael's not the only one who's sick. Quite a few of the children, plus some adults, have it. I'm afraid we're in for an epidemic. The sanitary conditions in this place are to be blamed. I'll speak to General Scott to see what the army is going to do for us. The sick ones must be isolated and given protection from the sun. This place could turn into a prison of death."

John shivered. He had heard about smallpox epidemics. Even with the best of conditions, many people died. The Cherokee had little genetic resistance to the disease. Rachael was a full blood. What chance did she have?

Worchester saw the troubled, searching look on John's face. "The government that shut your people in this stockade is responsible for any who die," he said. "Man's inhumanity to man causes the suffering you see all around you. The government must not have planned to keep you in prison

111

this long or no doubt they would have provided better living conditions. You can't blame God for this. I think the prolonged drought has made travel impossible.''

"Then why doesn't God step in and do something? Why does He allow all this suffering?" John asked.

"Ah, the mystery of suffering." Worchester sighed. He took off his glasses, slowly polishing them on his handkerchief. "I wish I knew all the answers to that question." He sighed again. Then he spoke musingly, as though he had been thinking over the possible answers to this question many times himself. "I think there are many reasons God allows suffering. I know a few of them from experience, a few of them by faith, and some I'm sure I'll never know until I see my Lord. Why did God allow His own Son to suffer?" He looked questioningly at John.

John lifted an eyebrow quizzically and shook his head. "I don't know, sir."

Worchester rubbed his chin with a work-hardened hand. "The Bible says that Christ had to learn from experience what it was like to obey, even when obeying meant suffering. Through that experience He proved Himself perfect. Suffering is one way God uses to make a Christian grow in his faith. In suffering, if we turn to Christ for help, He will give us the strength we need. Suffering makes a Christian strong."

John felt the words seep into his mind. They were like cool water refreshing his thirsty spirit.

112

Looking intently at the tired, middle-aged pastor, John thought, *Here is a man who has chosen suffering for himself so he could help the Cherokee. He's a man who lives what he believes.* In John's eyes the little man stood very tall.

"What about all these people here who are not Christians?"

Worchester said firmly, "Every man under the sun faces suffering sometime in his life. Suffering is the end result of sin. Sometimes this suffering makes a man turn to Christ, as you did. Other men turn away from God, growing hard and bitter in their suffering. Look at Bold Hunter. John, I hope you will take every opportunity to tell Bold Hunter what Christ means to you. I'm really worried about him. He used to be a fine boy, but now he's full of hatred and bitterness. There was a time a while back when Bold Hunter was close to accepting Christ, but he turned away." Worchester's deep voice was sad. "The hatred in his life will destroy him if he doesn't turn to Christ."

John was silent. The pastor didn't know how much he was asking.

That evening, after the sun had set, the men without active cases of smallpox were locked as usual in the men's building. John cuddled Pris in his arms until she slept. Then he settled her on the floor next to him on his shirt. In the cover of darkness, he dropped to his knees to pray. He tried to get his mind off the suffocating heat, the bodies packed tightly around him, his maddening thirst, and his gnawing hunger. Although his lips were

113

silent, his heart was stretching toward God in his torment.

"O God, please get us out of this stinking prison. Give me freedom—freedom to walk beneath the trees without someone pointing a gun at me, to smell clean air, to be alone. I want to swim in our lake, to feel that cool water soothe my tortured body. I want to be where the crops are growing, to hear the slaves singing in the fields. I want to be free to ride Jasper like the wind until we're both out of breath. I want to walk into the cool library of my own home, to pick up a book and read, to eat when I'm hungry and to drink all I want. O God, take away this gnawing hunger and everlasting thirst. Set me free from the daily humiliation of begging for rations. Give me freedom from men who want to kill me." John's heart felt as if it were twisted into a tight knot, ready to burst with his intense longing for freedom. "O God," he continued. "I know You can't give me back all that was taken from me, but please give me the strength that You have promised in Your Word. I can't take much more of this, Father. You said You give power to the faint, and that to them that have no might, You increase their strength. I need that strength now, Lord."

John opened his eyes in despair. Nothing was changed. He still felt caged, trapped like a wild animal. The darkness was thick, heavy with humidity. His stomach ached with hunger, his gut with sickness. He was dried out, his tongue sticking to the roof of his mouth. Where was the help

114

that God had promised? They that wait on the LORD shall renew their strength; they shall mount up with wings as eagles; they shall run, and not be weary; and they shall walk, and not faint." The words echoed in his head. Timeless, eternal words. Words for him and for the millions of other people who had lived before him and those millions who would live after he was gone. Promises to the Cherokee and the white man, to any man. God, the Creator, promised strength to any who would wait on Him. "Thank You, Father, for Your promises," John whispered.

Somewhere to the left, in the darkness, came muffled sobs. A small boy was trying manfully not to cry. Perhaps his father lay outside with smallpox. It was a terrifying cry, the tone hopeless. That stiffled sobbing had an almost instantaneous effect. All over the room young voices began to sniffle or moan. John's heart went out to the children.

Because the Cherokee are a musical people, they sing at weddings, births, deaths, while working the land, at the spinning wheel, rocking the cradle, pounding the corn, and during their festivals. With or without excuse they sing. So it was natural for John to turn to song, trying to comfort the boys. He chose the text which Reverend Worchester had preached that morning:

> Peace I leave with you,
> Peace I leave with you,
> My peace give I unto you,

Let not your heart be troubled,
Neither let it be afraid.
Peace I leave with you.

Quickly catching the simple melody led by John's rich baritone, men and boys joined the singing. The wonder and truth of the words encircled the room. Yes, there was still the darkness, the heat, the stench, the loneliness, and the longing for home, but there was also peace in many hearts.

"Please, let's sing some more," a very young voice begged. "My mother always used to sing me to sleep." Pastor Worchester led in singing a psalm of praise. John had a feeling that the singing would become a nightly service, transforming the worst hour of the day into a time of fellowship.

Just before falling into a deep sleep, a thought wormed its way into his mind. *The strength to endure comes as we reach out to help others.*

The next morning a small lad shuffled shyly over to John as he sat on the ground outside the men's building. John was thinking about Pris. Lately she was always so quiet and seldom laughed except when she was playing in the river. She only cried now when she was badly frightened. And she didn't even ask for her momma anymore. She seemed content just to be near John. Whenever she was awake, she clung to him and woke instantly if he tried to put her down when she was sleeping.

The boy stood a minute or two in front of John,

116

head down, bare toe digging in the dirt. John looked up absently.

"Will you tell me about Jesus?" The child's grin was shy.

"Sure, sit down and we'll talk man to man," John said, gladness tinging his voice.

Before he knew what was happening, about twenty boys ranging in age from six to about twelve had followed the small lad and were sitting in a semicircle facing John. Hero worship shone on every dirty face.

Looking at the thin, ragged youngsters, John's heart was sore. *They're so young and vulnerable,* he thought. *How can I help these little ones face the heat and hunger? It's more than a man can bear. How can a child?*

John told them what they needed to hear: the eternal story of God's love. They sat quietly in the blazing heat, eyes scrunched tight against the white light. A dull hopelessness, making their faces look far older than their years, slowly slid away as their minds responded to the story of Jesus' love.

John was finished. He didn't know what else to tell them. They still sat looking at him with expectant faces. A boy about seven, both front teeth missing, scooted closer. Across his nose was a generous sprinkling of freckles, and his light yellow hair stuck out like straw. His big brown eyes were serious when he said, "I want to ask Jesus to come into my life. Will you pray with me?"

John bowed his head, amazed at their quick

117

understanding. The boy prayed out loud, asking Jesus to come into his life and forgive his sins. A murmur of voices joined his as some of the other little ones became children of God.

When the boy raised his head, his face sparkled and he was grinning from ear to ear. "Thanks, mister," he said. John wet his dry lips and tried to whistle. The little fellow tried, too, but his missing teeth kept him from mimicking his hero. John's lips were so dry and cracked, he couldn't whistle either. They laughed together.

"Uh, Mr. Ross." It was the oldest boy in the group, a dark lad with troubled black eyes. "Are Indians not as good as white men?" he asked.

John's sensitive mouth curved into a grim smile. This was one of the problems he had been facing himself. It was hard not to feel inferior when one was treated like an animal, and some of the soldiers had made the situation even worse with their name-calling. "If God is willing to live in your heart, then you must be pretty precious to Him," John said. "What does it matter what anyone else thinks?"

The troubled look left the boy's eyes. "That's right! Thank you, sir." He walked away toward his mother with his head held high.

"What's your name?" John asked the boy who had prayed aloud. The others had all left.

"Sitting Bear's my Indian name. Mom calls me Jamie."

"Jamie, we're brothers in Jesus now. You can

118

come to me anytime you need help. Pris, say 'Hi' to your new brother.''

Pris smiled a slow smile that lighted her face. "Jesus wove me," she said. John knew he would never forget that moment.

10

Someone was dead. A crowd of people gathered near Pastor Worchester as he hammered a sign on the stockade doors. John knew the Cherokee custom. When someone died during the night, a notice was tacked on the church door at sunrise and the church bell was rung.

Here there was no bell to ring. A low wailing moan sent spasms of dread through John. He jerked to his feet. He ran through the stockade clearing toward the notice, praying, "Not Rachael, O God, please not Rachael." Fear for her life prickled his skin.

The stench of death lay heavy in the still, hot air. John could see four bodies covered by a blanket on the dirt. He pushed his way through the crowd to read the notice.

Sarah Raincrow—age four years
Tim Takatokoh—age six months
Samuel Echohawk—age ten years
Mary Matthews—age nineteen years
Baby Matthews—unborn

Rachael was still alive! John turned away from

the pitiful heap of bodies. He had to go somewhere where he could be alone. *But there's no place to be alone in this prison. Everywhere I go, someone is already there.* He went blindly toward the wall, his lips clamped into a tight line, a greenish tinge around his mouth. He leaned against the fence, then slid slowly to the ground. Resting his head in both hands, the sickness churned inside.

Those still mounds under that tattered blanket had been happy, carefree children. He remembered when they were chubby, full of life and health. Sammy Echohawk had always said, "When I get big like you, John, I'm going to have a horse just like Jasper." *He had so much determination, I really thought he would own a good horse one day, even though his family wasn't well off,* John thought.

Little Sarah Raincrow had been the pride of her family. Such a bright, inquisitive child. Always asking questions. When anything was going on, from playing ball to learning to weave, Sarah had been Johnny-on-the-spot, asking her endless questions. *The last time I saw her in her own home,* John thought, *she was standing by her mother and older sister, listening to the hum of the spinning wheel and the smack of the loom. They were weaving some special material for Sarah's birthday dress.*

He shook himself and stood up, resting his hot forehead against the smooth timber of the stockade wall. His face was twisted in pain. Smashing

121

his fist into the stockade wall, he was glad for the pain. "Why, God, why?" he asked. "They were so innocent. Why do the innocent suffer?"

Pris lifted her little arms, cupped her tiny hands around John's face, and kissed him. Then she put her arms around his neck and hugged him.

John's anger faded as he cuddled his baby sister. He buried his face in the chubby folds of her soft white neck. Her golden hair tickled his nose. *If only I could get her out of this prison of death.*

Bold Hunter's voice sounded like the hissing of a snake, "What's wrong *Unaka* [white man], you God no help?"

John spun around to face the young Indian. "I don't know much about God, but I *do* know that somewhere He has the answer. What kind of answer do *you* have for all this?" John waved an expressive arm toward the bodies, the filth, the prison.

Bold Hunter's eyes flashed. "Thunder man no come for long time. He protect Cherokee. Me go to long man [river]. Have water prayer for people. Face east on bank of flowing long man. Wash in long man. Pray. Lay on bank long time. Have dream. Blue [disaster] covering Cherokee go away. White [serenity, joy] come. Hear drumbeats far away. Get louder and louder in head. Drumbeats stir in blood, in bones. Now drums in air, all around, very loud. Drums make Bold Hunter stand tall. Put on war paint. Make war dance. Women make whoop for me. War food is tasted. Put away. Me take war trail, take bow, hatchet, long rifle, knife, get scalps. Avenge Cherokee dead.'' Bold Hunter's voice had risen in triumph; he held his head high. John almost could picture him leading a war party against the white soldiers.

But John knew what Bold Hunter didn't. For every white man killed, there were twenty who could take his place. The Cherokee were hopelessly outnumbered. And fighting would not bring back the innocent dead.

With hundreds of Indians sick with smallpox, the trip to the Oklahoma Territory was being delayed until cooler weather. Each morning a new list of the dead was tacked to the stockade door, sometimes with as many as twenty names on it. Jamie Sitting Bear and Grandfather Raincrow had made the list.

The sick were isolated in a large area where crude blanket and birch bark shelters had been built by the Indians to protect them from the sun. John's mother and six other women were nursing the sick day and night. Each morning soldiers removed the dead bodies and buried them in a sizable cemetery which had sprung up just ouside the walls. Except for double rations of water, the soldiers gave no other help, staying as far away from the prisoners as possible. The few who ventured inside had had the dread disease in their childhood.

"Good news, John!" boomed Pastor Worchester one day. "Rachael's improved. She's been sick over three weeks, and most of those who die don't last that long. Her pox are dried up and starting to fall off, so I think she's going to make it."

John flashed a smile, his first since Jamie Sitting Bear had decided for Jesus.

The pastor continued to talk. "This morning Rachael sat up alone. She's thin and wobbly, but she's definitely starting to recuperate."

"That's good news, sir. I really didn't think she had much chance. How does she look? I mean, is she scarred?"

"Her skin's as smooth and clear as a newborn child's. She told me she had prayed that if God spared her, that He would also keep her from being pockmarked."

"I can't wait to see her." *Why do some people live and others die?* he wondered. *Why are some prayers answered, but not all? It's more than I can figure out. Sure glad Rachael knows how to get her prayers answered.*

A week later John sent word to Rachael to pray for Pris. The little girl had a raging fever and couldn't even keep milk down. She lay limp in John's arms, her big blue eyes full of bewilderment.

"Let me nurse her, Mother. She likes me to sing to her," John pleaded with his mother when she came for the baby.

His mother's face was haggard, with dark rings circling her eyes. Her dress was torn and her blonde hair uncombed. A wistful smile, a light kiss on John's cheek, then she said, "No, dear, a mother needs to be with her child when she is sick." Reluctantly, John gave Pris up.

Charity came to him early the next morning. John was sitting hunched with his head in his hands just outside the men's building. He was expecting her. "Did Pris suffer, mother?" he asked hoarsely when she knelt beside him. Charity took both his hands in her cold ones.

"No, darling. She was sleeping. She woke up with a bright laugh, like she used to at Pleasant Acres, you remember. I think she thought she was back in her own crib because she asked for her baby bear. Then she smiled, closed her eyes, and said, 'Tell John night.' Then she was gone."

In the days that followed, John felt like part of his own body had been amputated. He was so accustomed to having Pris with him. He saw her slow smile in shafts of sunlight under the trees. A whispered breeze across the back of his neck reminded him of her sweet breath when she hugged him. Many times he stopped himself short of pointing out a pretty butterfly or flower to her. She was gone. He missed her. *Does one suffer the anguish of loss in order to be filled with His love?* he thought. *If we had no pain, we would need no Spirit of Christ to comfort us.*

11

October 1, 1838, was a day John would never forget. The stockade doors opened for the last time. His spirits were high since the forced inactivity was finally ending. Pausing beside the graveyard, he took a final look at Pris's grave. "How can such an impersonal plot of ground contain our sunny little girl?" he said aloud. "But she's not really there," he reminded himself. Still, he hated to leave her there alone.

Charity's eyes were full as John put an arm around her, guiding her away from the cemetery toward the wagons. "Mom, one of those fifty Conestoga wagons will be our home for the next six months or so. They're not very big, nor very comfortable, but they'll get us out of here." Charity smiled bravely through her tears. "Wherever we are together will be home. We'll do the best we can with what we have. The water kegs strapped to the sides are dripping, so we should have fresh water today. Do you think we'll get more food than we had in prison?"

John walked over to look inside a wagon. "Some barrels, bags, and boxes are inside," he said. "But they don't look very promising. There can't be room enough for more than ten people, and it doesn't look like there are enough wagons for all of us. I don't see any blankets or bedding either." Disappointment tinged his voice.

"At least cooler weather has finally come," Rachael commented as she looked anxiously at the sky. When the drought had ended, cooler weather brought gray overcast skys. Dark clouds, scattered across the sky, foretold rain. A hazy blue mist hung low over the Smokies, so that the lower range was barely discernible. The higher ranges were blurred in the smoky mist.

"We can plan on getting the last wagon," John said with resignation. "Ben McDonal's assigning wagons." He was right. It was almost noon before all the wagons were assigned and loaded. "Leave it to the army to work with efficiency." John's sarcastic voice was loud enough for the wagon master to hear.

But McDonal was in a good mood and ignored the jab. "We ain't got enough injuns left to help navigate your wagon, pup," he told John with a smirk on his face. "You and thet vermint there'll have to git this wagon to the Oklahoma Territory by yourselves." He nodded his head in the direction of Bold Hunter, who had kept out of sight until Rachael was assigned a wagon.

John's heart sank. Would the man never get his fill of tormenting him? All the other wagons had four to five men to get them across the mountains, and their job would be hard enough. But it would be impossible for two.

Mrs. Ross and Rachael were crowded into the wagon with sixteen Indian children, all of whom had lost their parents in the smallpox epidemic. John groaned when he looked inside. Rachael and his mother were sitting on the hard boards with children on their laps. The other children were so heaped together that he couldn't tell who was on top and who was on the bottom. They were jammed in like so many pickles in a jar. It was going to be a very uncomfortable ride.

"We are out of the wind," Mrs. Ross said. "That's one thing for which to be thankful. Let's all pray for John," she told the children. "He needs warmer clothes, and there just aren't any to be found."

Looking up, John saw the rain moving down the mountain toward them in great waving sheets. The wind came gusting into the valley, shaking the tree branches, rustling the dry leaves, and bringing the rain.

"You drive," McDonal commanded, pointing a thick forefinger at Bold Hunter. The young Indian scrambled up onto the wagon seat. He unwound the reins from the whip socket with unaccustomed fingers. John showed him how to hold the reins and signal the four oxen. "You walk!" McDonal yelled to John over the wind. "Don't need any more weight on that wagon." With a look of suppressed anger on his face, John jumped down.

The rain hit them with pounding suddenness. Yelling above the wind, McDonal said, "I hope you don't push your guts out getting this wagon over these mountains. I got other plans for you. When things get boring, I'm gonna have me some fun. In the meantime, you're gonna walk and push and wish you was dead!" The veins in his neck stood out as he roared with glee. Mounting a big roan horse, he looked at John with a twisted smirk. When he lifted his bullwhip, the hair on the back of John's neck stood up. With a crack that opened a red stripe across the lead ox's rump he bellowed, "Wagon, ho!"

The wagons were rolling. Children leaned out the back into the rain, waving good-bye with their hands. The wagons lumbered slowly away from the stockade. The Cherokee nation was leaving its homeland. As the wagons jolted past several hundred freshly dug graves outside the stockade, tears filled many eyes. Parents, brothers, and sisters were being left behind in those graves.

Charity Ross buried her face in her hands as they passed the tiny grave with the wooden cross on which John had carved the words, "Safe in the Arms of Jesus." She circled her empty arms around an Indian child, clutching him to her aching heart. They clung to each other, crying.

The sadness of the journey was shared by the elements as the sky wept. Chill October rain fell in torrents, turning the clay bloodred.

Soaked through, John shivered in his thin muslin shirt. With his long blond hair plastered to his head, the driving rain in his eyes, he could barely see Bold Hunter inexpertly driving the oxen. With the ruts in the road already flooded with water, John's bare feet kept slipping in the mud.

On the right they passed the Moravian Brethren Mission. So John knew they were at Springplace on the road from Georgia to west Tennessee, three miles east of the Connesaga River. John had not attended the mission, but he knew some of the Indian youngsters who had. They were taught reading, writing, arithmetic, English, grammar, and geography. The girls had been, John reminded himself, taught spinning, sewing, knitting, and how to make their own stockings. The boys had learned farming, how to make clothing, to use the wheel and card to make cotton cloth, and to guide the horse and plow.

John had to be careful that the army officers riding beside the train didn't ride him down. They were as anxious to be on the move as he was. The horses splashed and slipped through the mud, trotting up and down the creeping wagon train. Their muzzle-loading rifles were primed and ready, lying across their saddles as though they expected every Indian man on the train to venture an escape. *Who would ever try it?* John thought grimly, *with one able-bodied soldier armed to the teeth for every two weakened Cherokee men on the train.* He eyed with envy the full-length yellow oilskins the soldiers wore.

Already he could tell some of the militiamen had been jugging whiskey to ward off the cold. *They'll be dead drunk by tonight,* he mused. *They'd better leave our women alone.*

The rain slashed into his face from the west. *Land of the dead,* he thought. The rain beat so loudly in his ears that he could scarcely hear the friendly creaking of the wagon with its wet canvas slapping against the sides. John kept his eyes on the oxen, patiently straining their shoulders against the loaded wagon. With their heads hanging down and their ears fallen forward, they were blindly following the wagon ahead.

Ten feet behind John's wagon rode several regiments of cavalry. The tall blue hat emblazoned with the eagle of the United States was their only identifying mark as they, too, were covered from head to toe with yellow oilskin. The jangle of their spurs, an occasional clank of a sword, along with the sound of many men on horseback robbed John of any feeling of freedom he might have hoped for.

Overheard snatches of their conversation, bits of jokes flung his way by the wind, and ribald songs meant to cheer them, only made him feel lonely, cut off from human companionship. But at least he heard the news that they were headed for Rattlesnake Springs, Tennessee.

John swung his arms. Hunched against the wind, he couldn't keep from shivering. "I've never been so miserably cold in my life. Even the blasting heat of the stockade was better than this. Lord, if You don't give me strength, I'll never make it to Oklahoma."

They had been walking for hours in the heavy rain. The mud sucked at his feet, making every step a contest of strength. After lying around in that prison with insufficient food for five months, this kind of exercise was utterly exhausting.

Ahead the wagons were bumping over wood. The oxen's hooves clanged softly. *A covered bridge. Must be the Chickamauga River. We'll soon be in Tennessee. That mountain on the other side of the river is going to be tough getting over.*

John stood beneath the protection of the covered bridge as long as he dared. Finally the horsemen forced him on. The road began to narrow as mountains rose closely on both sides. The wagon in front was being pushed by four Indians, and they were not having an easy time. Slowly the wagon moved up the steep ascent and began to circle the mountain.

Ruts which had been cut deeply into the dirt from the preceding wagons were now flooded. John's wagon started up the steep slope, then ground to a stop. "Put your shoulder to it, whelp!" The roar of Ben McDonal's voice cut through the dense rain. He had sloshed back through the muck to check on John. There he was sitting on his big horse, grinning down.

Grinding his teeth with the effort, John grasped the slippery spoke of the wagon wheel and shoved. The wagon inched upward. Bold Hunter handed the reins to Rachael, his black eyes burning holes into McDonal. Grabbing a spoke of the other wheel, together he and John pushed and shoved the heavy wagon as it ground slowly through the ruts, inching up the mountain.

Opening the flap at the back of the wagon, Charity asked anxiously, "Do you want the children and us to get out and walk? I really don't think you two can get this wagon up."

"No, Mother, you and the children stay inside," John answered, breathing hard. "We don't want you all to get wet. We'll get this wagon up somehow."

Charity frowned anxiously at her son. He was drenched, and so thin. With his clothes plastered down, she could see how much weight he had lost. His shoulders looked extra wide compared to the leanness of his body. Surely he would catch pneumonia standing barefoot in the rain. Tears stood in her eyes as she mentally compared this shivering bedraggled youth to the well-dressed son ready to leave for Princeton. He didn't have any of the trappings of wealth now, but he did have a firmer line to his jaw than before. The deep blue eyes were calm; steadiness had replaced the look of reckless daring. The cocky arrogance she remembered was missing. Reassured by the look of inner strength she saw, she closed the flap.

The two young men grunted as they pushed and shoved the heavy wagon, inching it up the steep road. John's head was reeling and his ears buzzing with the effort. Then the front wheels hung up and the wagon wouldn't move at all. Ben McDonal sat on his horse and laughed, his tone deadly.

"You got a long way to go, Ross. One way or another, you ain't never gonna make it to Oklahoma. You'll regret the day you ever tangled with big Ben McDonal." With a vicious spur he sent his horse on up the mountain. John was too cold and tired to care. He almost wished Ben would shoot him.

John rubbed his raw shoulder. His hands were slippery with mud. He leaned against the wagon, catching his breath. "I'm not going to push my insides out on this thing," he told Bold Hunter. "Either we get help, or we just sit here," he said grimly.

A soldier covered in oilskin dismounted from his horse and took a place between the two youths. The three strained against the wagon until with a lurch it moved on up the mountain.

Needing a breather, they stopped to rest. "Don't I know you from somewhere?" John asked the helpful soldier. "You look familiar."

The man in oilskin was short, about five feet nine, but strongly built. Red hair hung limp and wet beneath his hat. He had a frank, honest face, good-looking in a rugged way. "Nope, don't think so. I'm from Massachusetts. Just got here to police the removal. Regiment got in last night. Name's Jeremy. Jeremy Worchester." The soldier's voice was a younger version of Pastor Sam's.

"That explains it!" John's voice was excited. "Sam Worchester's a friend of mine. He said he had a son a little older than I. Sam did say you were in the army, but I don't think he knew you were coming here."

"Nope, our orders were secret. Most folks in America are riled up about this removal. General Wool resigned his commission because of it. 'Old

134

Fuss and Feathers' took his place. People think the removal is un-American. Don't like it."

"I'm honored to meet you," John said, "and much obliged for your helping us like this." In a lower voice he continued, "Guess you noticed McDonal's been riding me pretty hard. I hope you don't get in trouble with him for helping us."

"Don't worry about McDonal. The saddle will be on the other horse when the wagon conductor gets wind of this. I've been anxious to see my sister again. She's on the wagon train, too, I hear. Have you met her?"

Interest flickered through John's mind along with an uncomfortable feeling of embarrassment. "Yes," he replied.

"She wants to help Dad and the Cherokees in any way she can," Jeremy went on. "Say, you sure don't look like a Cherokee. Are you?"

"Uh huh. My dad was an eighth. My uncle is the chief." John would have preferred not to have to answer that question so often. It brought to mind too many things that he didn't want to sort out or think about.

A mounted soldier yelled, "Hey, Jeremy, get going! The others are leaving this wagon behind. Let's close the gap."

"Come and help then," he answered. "We need at least four men on this wagon."

The soldier grumbled. "Always asking someone to do something he don't want to do." Nevertheless, he dismounted and took a place beside Jeremy.

John was exhausted. Would they ever reach the top of this mountain? Just before nightfall he could feel the muddy ground beneath his cold feet begin to level off. Wagons were halted, and camp was being made on the narrow, twisting road. There was no other place to go.

The rain continued, sometimes slowing to a drizzle, but mostly it was driving hard, like cold slivers, into John's flesh. It was impossible to build a fire.

John found the inside of the Conestoga damp and chilly. He and Bold Hunter hungrily consumed cold hominy grits while they sat on the front seat. The women and children remained in the wagon, cramped and restless.

In the deepening dusk, the soldiers pitched their tents on any flat spots they could locate. They climbed into their bedrolls and ate their rations. John noticed that a heavy guard had been posted. Obviously they didn't want to lose any Indians on such a wild night.

John unhitched the oxen, hobbling them so they could graze. He looked at Bold Hunter. "Where do we sleep?" he asked, his teeth chattering. Bold Hunter pointed beneath the wagon bed. John looked dubiously at the wet mud. Water was dripping off the wagon like a miniature waterfall. Only the center would offer scant protection.

They cut fir branches with their knives, making a bed beneath the wagon. Some they laid over themselves as a sort of wet blanket. The wind howled unhindered here at the crest of the mountain. The temperature was falling.

Once inside the fir boughs, it was a relief to be out of the wind and rain, but it was terribly cold. John lay between the still dripping branches and shivered. His teeth kept chattering despite his best efforts to still their rhythm. His legs felt as if they ended in lumps of ice.

Overhead the rustling in the wagon stopped, and he thought of his mother sleeping in the damp, crowded wagon. John was too exhausted to sleep. *I don't know which is worse,* he pondered, *the drumming of the rain or Bold Hunter's snoring.* In the distance a single wolf voiced a dismal howl, echoing the heaviness in John's heart.

Lifting heavy eyelids, he heard it again. The bugle. Time to rise and shine. It wasn't even light out. John groaned. Another day full of rain. Around him soldiers grudgingly started making movements of beginning the day. Everything smelled musty. John's clothes were still damp. A hot bath and steak and eggs sounded so good. It seemed like years ago when he used to take them for granted. Now he didn't know whether to rub his stomach or his feet. One rumbled; the others were numb. Waiting until the last possible minute, he crawled stiffly out from beneath the wagon. A vigorous warm-up got his circulation going.

The soldiers cursed and grumbled as they saddled their horses for another hard day's ride. "I sure didn't want to pull this duty," a nasal voice complained. "You can say what you want, but I

137

say a terrible wrong's being done to these ignorant savages. We ain't got any rights to make them leave this land."

"Yeah, but what can we do?" came the sullen answer. "We're under orders. When old Dan Webster failed, what can a poor private in this man's army do?"

After John hitched the oxen, he bolted down more cold hominy grits. "I'm sorry, but this is the best we can do," Rachael said, apologizing for the scant food. She ladled John some water from the barrel tied in the corner of the wagon.

"Did you sleep well, John? Were you dry?" his mother asked. "I worried about you all night." Deep creases were etched between her eyebrows.

"Sure, Mother. The fir branches kept me warm," John answered gallantly. Rachael looked at the lines of weariness around his mouth and eyes, but said nothing.

His mother smiled, partially convinced. "The children were cold. We need blankets. Don't you think the army will issue us some?"

"I'll ask, Mother." He told her about Jeremy Worchester.

In the distance, the bugle sounded for the wagons to roll. Bold Hunter climbed into the driver's seat, singing out in a strong voice, "Ho!"

John walked. At least he wouldn't have to push going downhill.

From the plateau where they had camped, the distant mountaintops were just visible through the cold drizzle. Clouds hung low over the road. In

138

spots, thick fog made driving dangerous and its dampness penetrated into the marrow of John's bones. The cold settled in with an ache. He coughed a deep, dry cough.

The wagon began its descent, but it was too steep. Too late, Bold Hunter grabbed the wooden brake, slamming it down hard. It pulled hard on the left rear wheel. Sliding with incredible speed sideways over the slippery mud, the wagonload of people headed for the steep drop-off.

12

With all the speed he could muster, John raced toward the right lead oxen. Stamping and snorting, the bewildered animal obeyed repeated commands to "Gee," as John pulled the nose ring to the right. The other oxen followed. The weight of the wagon pulled the oxen back toward the brink. John pulled both nose rings, urging the lead animals to strain against the wagon. It was all over in a few seconds. The wagon was stopped, its left rear wheel spinning crazily as it dangled over the edge of the gorge. The oxen and wagon stood crosswise on the narrow road.

In the excitement John automatically took charge, resuming his role as overseer without thinking. He ordered, "Jeremy, take the ox reins and keep these animals steady so they don't move backward. You other men get over here and help me get this wagon back on the road." The tone of command in his voice spurred the men into action. "Mother, you and the children move slowly to the front of the wagon, then get out. Don't panic. Everything's under control."

Bold Hunter was green around the edges of his mouth as he carefully leaped down from the driver's seat. The children jumped eagerly down from the wagon into the rain, hopping and bolting about in their excitement. John held Rachael in one arm and Mrs. Ross in the other while they clung to him in relief. Rachael whispered huskily, "We'd all be dead if it hadn't been for your quick action."

Bold Hunter's eyes smoldered. He looked as if he wanted to take John apart, limb from limb, and hang the remains on the nearest tree.

Using ropes and manpower, the wagon was soon eased back onto the road. The wheel was bent a bit but still usable, so the women and children scrambled back inside. The excited babble of voices continued during much of the day.

After the near accident, John noticed that the soldiers were looking at him with more respect. Maybe they didn't think he was such an ignorant savage now. But it worried him to see the looks they cast in the direction of the wagon. Now they were aware of Rachael too.

He looked in the wagon to see if they were ready. "Thanks for saving our lives." Rachael's voice was hard to hear over the hubbub. In his soft, slow accent of the Georgian highlands, John answered, "My pleasure, ma'am." Even soaking wet, she was beautiful as she sat surrounded by the excited children. He could have stood there all day while she looked at him like that.

"Come on, Don Juan, get your medal of bravery and come on out here," Jeremy called. "We've got to get going."

141

John grinned. He jumped lightly onto the driver's seat saying to Bold Hunter, "I'll drive; this is no place for you to learn. Sit here and watch if you like." Bold Hunter sat watching John in smoldering silence.

The oxen plodded slowly down the narrow mountain road. Just before the next twist, John skillfully applied the brake. The job of getting the wagon down the steep mountain road, slippery with mud, many times obliterated by dense fog, and through the driving rain, left him physically drained. At the bottom he stopped the team to rest.

Supper was a repeat of the night before. Afterward John hurried out into the descending darkness to find Jeremy. On the way he made plenty of noise so that no trigger-happy guard would think he was trying to escape. Jeremy had pitched his tent beneath an outcropping rock and had hobbled his horse close by. He lay snug and dry inside his tent, eating his rations.

"Have some," he said, offering to share them with John.

"Thanks." John was quick to take the food. After he had feasted on cold jerky, beans, and cornbread, he asked, "Do you think the army can supply us with some blankets? The women and children are cold." He sat with his back hunched against the driving rain.

"I doubt that the army has any extra blankets, but I'll inquire," Jeremy replied. "Meanwhile, take my greatcoat to them. It should help warm a few." He rubbed his square chin thoughtfully.

"I'll wager my sister stocked her wagon with blankets. Tomorrow morning I'll trot over to her wagon to see. Been wanting to pay her a visit anyway, but just haven't had the opportunity."

"Much obliged." John coughed. He was glad he hadn't had to suggest that Jeremy go to Hope's wagon for blankets. "I best be getting back."

Next morning a heaviness had settled into John's chest and his hands were blue with cold as he fumbled while hitching the oxen. He was dragging with fatigue.

The rain had slackened to a light drizzle, and in the east a lightening sky promised clearing. Bold Hunter seemed unaffected by the rain as he sat ramrod straight next to the driver's seat. John climbed up wearily to begin the day's trek.

His spirits lifted when he saw Jeremy ride by, waving in salute as he passed. *He sits a horse well,* John thought. *How jaunty he looks, even in his oilskin.* He watched the soldier for a long time as his horse trotted briskly along the valley road toward the middle of the wagon train.

The drizzle stopped eventually, and shafts of sunlight shone here and there through the haze. Bold Hunter jumped to the ground for some exercise. John was savoring the clean smell of the air in his nostrils. Even after the rain, the land still bore testimony to the long drought. The summer's flowers were long since faded, grass was dried brown and hard. Only the yellow of the yarrow and the white Queen Anne's lace provided color

143

among the sun-dried grasses. Rachael peeped out the front flap.

"Come on out and sit by me," John invited. "I'll show you how to drive, in the event you ever need to."

Rachael didn't need any coaxing. She sat close to John as he held her hands in his, teaching her how to hold the reins and signal the oxen. Her hands warmed his cold ones. The sun burst forth in early morning glory.

"You and Bold Hunter aren't very friendly," Rachael said pointedly.

"No, not very. It's a rather delicate situation. Seems we both like the same girl."

Rachael blushed.

"Have you and he come to an understanding?" John didn't believe in climbing around a tree.

Rachael was quiet a long time. Then in a thoughtful voice she answered, "I've known him most of my life. He's very attractive. He's strong and wise, as well as kind." John began to think they were not talking about the same person. "He reads and writes Cherokee fluently. He's an excellent hunter, and he knows how to farm. He owned a nice farm close to the mission house. And he wants me to be his wife."

John sat looking intently at his hands, still holding hers. He muttered, "Do you want to marry him?"

"I can't, of course. He's not a Christian." Rachael had a slight catch in her husky voice.

144

John glanced at Rachael's averted face in surprise. "Why not?"

"Jesus said we are not to yoke ourselves with unbelievers," she answered sadly.

"Does Bold Hunter know that's the reason you won't marry him?" John asked abruptly.

"No. I don't want him to become a Christian to marry me. I want him to become a Christian because he knows he needs Jesus as his Saviour. Besides," Rachael said softly, "I'm not really sure I want to marry Bold Hunter."

Feeling a surge of joy, John put his arm around her.

"Ho, John. We brought the blankets." Jeremy's voice cut into their private world. His horse was laden with four large blankets. Beside him rode Hope on a dainty gray Appaloosa mare. She wore a rich-looking dark green riding habit that reflected the emerald green of her eyes. Bright red gold hair cascaded over her shoulders.

Looking across at her regal figure, John realized anew the poor condition of his own clothes. They were almost dry, but were caked with red muck. His long hair was matted down around his neck, while his dirty bare feet stuck out in front of the driver's seat with embarrassing nakedness.

Hope ignored him. Giving a slight formal nod to Rachael, she sat stiffly, motionless in her sidesaddle. Jeremy stared at her aloofness in bewilderment. John tightened his arm around Rachael, keeping both of her hands in his free one. After an awkward silence, Hope's eyes, full of her

145

vexation, flicked over John. He gave her his most ferocious look.

"I'm aware this is rather presumptuous of me, Miss Worchester, but didn't I part my hair this morning to your satisfaction?" Sarcasm was heavy in John's voice.

"I really am not at all concerned about the manner in which you did or did not part your hair, Mr. Ross," Hope replied, speaking the words slowly and distinctly, like icicles tinkling in the winter wind. "I merely made this call to offer you some warm clothes, but I notice that you've found other methods of keeping warm."

Rachael blushed and tried unsuccessfully to release herself from John's grip.

"Miss Worchester, may I present Miss Whiteswan." John's eyes were as full of steel as a gun barrel, his Georgian drawl coldly impersonal.

Hope's face softened. "I am pleased to meet you, Miss Whiteswan. My father has mentioned you many times in a most favorable way. I hope *we* can become good friends."

Rachael smiled faintly. Her reply was not so amicable. "It's an honor to meet you, Miss Worchester."

With a puzzled look from Hope to John, Jeremy tossed some blankets onto John's lap. "Here's a blanket for you and one for Bold Hunter, two more for those in the wagon. Keep my greatcoat as well. I can manage without it."

Hope smiled and then nodded her good-bye to Rachael, her cameo face set in a creamy mask.

146

Handing her bundle to Jeremy, without a further word she wheeled her horse and galloped away. Mud from her horse's hooves splattered John. He looked like Mount Vesuvius about to erupt.

Jeremy spoke to no one in particular. "What in tarnation got her so riled?" He rubbed a hand through his thick red hair, looking quizzically at John. "She had her claws out, but you sure had your spurs dug in. I don't know who was scratching the hardest. You didn't tell me you were such good friends."

John looked stonily at an ox's rump. Jeremy shot the bundle of clothes toward him. They landed neatly on top of John's clenched fists. "Hope's been handing out clothes since she joined the wagon train. These were all that were left. I had a fancy she'd been saving these for someone special, since she had them hidden under her seat. Shows you how wrong a person can be." Jeremy thought it prudent to leave. "Duty beckons. You know where to find me if you have any other needs."

"Thank you, Jeremy. We really are appreciative of the blankets," Rachael said sweetly. Jeremy grinned, saluted her, and left.

Rachael sat stiffly beside John. "She's the most beautiful girl I've ever seen. You're attracted to her, aren't you?"

"Attracted! She's worse than an onion poultice on the skin. I'm attracted to her like I'm attracted to a she bear separated from her cubs."

"Um." Rachael picked up the bundle. She

147

opened it, taking each item out with rising excitement. "Here's a warm woolen shawl. It's for Charity, of course." John's anger ebbed. Rachael looked pleased as she shook out a heavy homespun long-sleeved shirt of robin egg blue. "She matched your eyes perfectly. It's certainly large enough. She really did save these for you. No doubt she had to shop a long time to find this particular shirt." Rachael took John's arm, hugging him in delight.

"Look, here are some buckskin britches, with the pelt turned inside. They're for someone very tall," she teased. "I wonder how she knew your size so well?"

John felt his neck redden. The color spread to his face until it flamed. There was nothing he could do about it. "Stop teasing, Rachael. How could she know if they're my size? I've never seen her enough for her to know." John's voice was rough.

"Here's a pair of tremendously large shoes. Are your feet really that big?" She enjoyed teasing John, for she had rarely seen him lose his poise. "What are these called, anyway?"

John tried to appear casual. "They're brogans. Like hiking boots, only better. Any socks?"

"Three pair of heavy socks," Rachael answered triumphantly, holding them up for inspection. "My, a person could get loads of goodies in these if they were hung by the chimney at Christmas." John couldn't help laughing.

"Don't just sit there shivering. Get into these warm clothes. I'll drive while you change." She poked him playfully in the ribs, her own shyness overcome by his embarrassment.

John jumped lightly off the slowly moving wagon. A couple hundred yards ahead a river meandered into some trees. A perfect spot for a quick bath and change of clothes.

The trees were farther from the road than he had thought. Shucking the muddy clothes, he stood knee-deep in the cold water. Behind him, a horse was breaking through the undergrowth.

A sudden knot of fear tightened his stomach. He knew the wagon train had passed on down the road. Was Ben McDonal coming to make good his threat of whipping him to death? He had been a fool to come alone, to put himself right into Ben's hands.

13

"You expecting a ghost or my sister?" Jeremy's bass voice was tinged with glee at John's startled expression.

Cold water splashed in his face was the answer.

"I thought you'd be wanting a bath," he went on, "so I brought you some soap. Government issue. But if that's all the thanks I get, I'll just take my soap and go." When he made as if to turn his horse and gallop away, John lunged after him, half pulling him from the saddle. "You've gotten me so wet now that I might as well have a quick wash too," Jeremy said, laughing as he dismounted then began undressing.

John never did tell Jeremy how glad he was to see his freckled face.

"Ow! Why didn't you tell me the water was so cold?" Jeremy howled as he stuck his big toe into the water, then backed away.

"Come on in, lily," John taunted. "It's spring-fed. Our rivers are always icy cold." He lathered himself with soap, splashing about to keep warm. Jeremy was forcing himself to walk knee-deep into the bone-chilling water when John suddenly slipped on a wet rock and fell. Jeremy burst into laughter at the picture he made sprawled across the rocky bed of the river. John grabbed Jeremy's ankle, jerking him down into the frigid water where they wrestled a few seconds until John started coughing. The water was too cold for roughhousing, but he stayed in until he had thoroughly washed his long hair.

Jumping out, they shook themselves like dogs before hustling into their dry clothes.

"Say now, you look like a civilized gentleman instead of a savage Injun." Jeremy looked approvingly at John's new clothes.

"You still look like a brutal soldier to me." John grinned. He took a long drink from a spring of ice-cold water bubbling up from the ground.

Jeremy sobered. "We don't like this job. Me especially. Gen'l Scott said this trip'll take about six months. I'll be mustered out of the army after that, and I'm planning to stay in the new territory to help your people get settled." He combed his hair with a pocket comb and then handed it to John. "God's called me to preach."

John was busy working the tangles out of his wet hair. "How can you be so sure?"

"Up until a couple of months ago, the last thing I wanted in the world was to be a preacher. I always hankered for adventure. Hey, don't break my comb! And there was part of me, too, that wanted to do the things I'd been taught not to do. So I joined the army." Jeremy's green eyes were looking at John, gauging his interest.

"What did your dad say?" John asked, trying to see his reflection in the stream.

"Dad always said," Jeremy struck a pose and mimicked his father's voice so well that John chuckled, "find out what God wants you to do, then do it. You won't ever be happy until you find God's will for your life." John could picture the elder Worchester advising his son.

Jeremy produced a fishing pole. John squatted on the grassy bank beside Jeremy, his flesh tingling from the cold bath. He felt relaxed and content. It was good to have a friend. "Did you find God's will for your life?" he asked. Jeremy took so long to answer that John stretched out on the ground with his hands laced under his head. Lazily he looked at the clear sky. The October sun had burned off the overcast. The air was crisp in John's lungs as he inhaled deeply the pungent scent of autumn. He had almost forgotten the question when Jeremy began to talk.

"I asked God what His will was for my life. I prayed about it a lot. The only trouble was," he knit his heavy red brows, "I never listened for His answer. Too busy planning what I wanted to do."

The brilliant gold red leaves rustled overhead. John's eyelids were heavy, and his eyes closed. His muscles jerked slightly as they relaxed. He murmured, "So what happened?"

"Got myself into a scrape. Started keeping company with the wrong crowd. Remember, now, I was looking for adventure. You don't find that in the army. Nothing but spit and polish, march and ride, routine jobs, maneuvers, saying yes, sir; no, sir; right away, sir. Got a bellyful in a hurry.''

John opened his eyes and looked at the strong profile of his friend. Apparently Jeremy wasn't too keen on continuing his story. He sensed that Jeremy seldom talked about himself. "C'mon, Yankee, don't be so reticent," John urged.

"Dad raised Hope and me strict. We never got away with mischief. Just work, study, and pray. He had a handful with us, though. I was always trying to run off and Hope had her own ways of getting around him." His lips curved into a smile as he remembered, then he looked a little grim. "Every time I ran off, he'd find me and bring me home and lick me until I thought it was just the natural way of life to have a stinging backside." John grinned, but Jeremy didn't.

"Don't misunderstand me. He is a good father, but it must have worried him that we didn't have a mother. She died when Hope was born. When I was a little shaver, I got his big black Bible. I was going to find that verse he was always quoting, "Spare the rod and spoil the child." I planned to slit it out with my knife, but I couldn't find it. In all likelihood, we needed most of the discipline.''

"I'll wager you did." It delighted John to think of Jeremy's proud-looking sister getting her bottom spanked.

"When I ran off and joined the army, he let me go. I was just a boy of sixteen. He bundled Hope off to a straitlaced girl's boarding school and came out here."

John wanted to hear more. "Army life was just as strict, except for off-duty hours. I made the most of them. I commenced drinking and gambling and doing everything else a man can think of, but I couldn't handle it. I woke up AWOL once after a night of revelry and spent some time behind bars. My temper was always getting me into fights. Then it would be off-hour duty. I came close to getting a dishonorable discharge before I regained my senses."

Jeremy sighed. His voice which had been matter-of-fact now held a tone of sorrow. "I had never let onto the others that I was a Christian. Three wasted years. The men were surprised when I started reading my Bible. At first they just jeered. Then they tried to get me mad. They'd hold me under cold showers or put manure in my bunk just before inspection. Sometimes they woke me in the middle of the night and forced me to clean the latrine. The sergeant always had a few choice jobs for me, but I was so glad to get back into fellowship with the Lord that I didn't care what they did. When they found they couldn't get to me, they started to ask questions." Jeremy's face lighted up like a harvest moon. "That's how I found the adventure I'd been looking for. The real jolt came whenever one of them decided he wanted to become a Christian. I got a peace in my heart that's more important to me than anything else." John nodded his head in understanding. He

154

felt that peace now and then. He'd like to have it all the time, but it seemed so elusive.

"Even though I hated the army, I decided to be a career man and witness to the soldiers the rest of my life. Then we got our orders to guard this removal. Dad said prayer, peace, and circumstances all guide a person into finding the will of God. God also added His still small voice." Jeremy leaned back against the grassy bank. This time he sighed with satisfaction. "Isn't God good?"

John looked down at his warm clothes. Then, mimicking Jeremy's clipped New England speech, he said, "Yep."

"We'd best get back to the wagon. You keep the trout for your wagonload to eat. Part of our job is to hunt and fish for the people," Jeremy added when John started to shake his head.

Jeremy looped his reins over his arm and walked back to the wagon train with John. "Who's the beautiful girl on the wagon? Your girl?" asked Jeremy casually.

John told him in sketchy form of Rachael's trouble with Ben McDonal, including McDonal's latest threat.

"That's some adventure," Jeremy said admiringly. "I wondered about those scars on your back. I'll keep my eyes on him. I can't report a threat to the CO, my commanding officer. We'll just have to sit tight until McDonal tries something again."

They walked past the mounted cavalry. "Next

time you decide to leave the wagon train, let me know," Jeremy said in an offhand way. "My CO takes a dim view of prisoners leaving unescorted."

John's blue eyes flashed and his mouth tightened as he said grimly, "So you just came to give me some soap, when all the time you were watching to see if I would try to escape."

"Don't be so peppery. We're friends. Someone has to guard you; it might as well be someone who likes your company. I won't be your guard in Oklahoma, but I'll still be your friend." Jeremy's clear green eyes pleaded for John to understand his position.

John's anger passed as suddenly as it had come. "Fine, Yankee," he drawled, "next time I take a fancy for a stroll, I'll play 'Yankee Doodle' on my drum."

At the wagon, Bold Hunter and Rachael were talking in Cherokee. John didn't like their intimate tête-á-tête. Bold Hunter acted as if Rachael was his intended. He was smiling tenderly, his mouth very close to hers. He had an animal magnetism about him that Rachael seemed attracted to.

"Make a nice couple, don't they?" Jeremy asked slyly.

"Decidedly, if in your opinion a panther and a deer make a nice couple," John said sourly. "I don't trust that panther."

"Looks like Rachael does," Jeremy pointed out.

John stood still, uncertain what he should do. *I don't want to make a scene in front of Rachael and*

156

haul the man down off the driver's seat, he thought. *She wants us to be friends. Sam wants me to witness to him. All I want to do is see the last of him.*

"Have Rachael clean the fish. I'll stay behind to guard her, and then we'll catch up."

John looked at Jeremy with a look that asked plainly, "Are you interested in her too?"

Jeremy's answering look just as plainly said, "No, I'm trying to show you I'm your friend."

Satisfied, John strode up to Rachael, handing her the fish. "Here's a surprise. Can you clean them?"

"You look so handsome!" her voice bubbled with pleasure. "The clothes are a perfect fit. All you need is a haircut." With her head tilted to the side, she surveyed him. "With a head like yours, even long hair looks good. You look like the master of Pleasant Acres."

John held up his arms to catch her. "Thank you, but this is nothing so fancy as that. Jump down. Jeremy has to stay with you." She was light in his arms.

"Bold Hunter stay also. Filet fish fast."

"Uh, I want to talk with you. This seems an appropriate time."

"Later." He flipped the reins toward John.

"Nope, only one Indian at a time can leave this wagon train," the crisp New England voice spoke up.

Bold Hunter sat back slowly. John could tell they hadn't fooled him. Bold Hunter knew they

157

had fabricated that scheme. He expected Bold Hunter to retaliate.

Swinging up onto the driver's seat, John grasped the reins. "Ho!" Bold Hunter started to get down.

"No, don't get down. I really do want to talk."

John didn't know how to begin. The silence became uncomfortable. He could feel Bold Hunter's antagonism and wondered if this was the wrong time. He licked his lips. *Why do I get myself into these situations? That's what Jeremy wanted when he concocted this plan. He wanted me to witness. Lord, I'll try. For You, not for him.* John's thoughts made him so uncomfortable, he squirmed. He rubbed his jaw.

Finally he asked bluntly, "You're not a Christian, are you?"

Bold Hunter's "No!" was designed to end the conversation.

Mentally John wiped his forehead. That was the wrong thing to say. How was he to get the conversation rolling? Bold Hunter simply sat like a wooden Indian.

"What's wrong with Christians?"

"Christians no have courage. Afraid. No take war trail. No take scalps. No fight soldiers." He turned a contemptuous face toward John. "Make friends with soldiers." He spoke like that crime was the height of treason.

"You're wrong. I'm not afraid to fight."

"Show Bold Hunter you no afraid. Then believe. *Unaka* eyes full of smoke, ears full of roaring water, mouth full of empty words. When Bold

Hunter see dead soldiers, believe Christians not afraid."

John's back stiffened at being called *Unaka;* nevertheless, he continued. "God can give you love for your enemies."

"Ha, ha, ha," Bold Hunter's laugh rang with contempt. "Jaybird sit on bush all day. Talk and talk. Who want to listen? You Christian, you scared!"

I'm not scared, but how can I prove it? John thought. *I don't want to kill anyone. How can I prove I'm not afraid to fight?*

14

Two shots reverberated some distance behind them. A quarter of the regiment behind the wagon wheeled their horses at the captain's command, galloping toward the shots.

Rachael needs help! "Whoa! Whoa there!" John stood up, pulling hard on the reins. Bold Hunter was out of the wagon before it had stopped moving. Three soldiers on horseback barred his way. "This is army business, Injun. Remain with the wagon."

John hit the ground running. Numerous soldiers surrounded him. For a minute he thought he would be trampled under their horses' hooves. "Get up there and keep that wagon moving!" He obeyed.

Craning his neck around the dust-covered canopy of the wagon, he strained to see. Behind the guard he glimpsed where the investigative company had turned off the road, but that was all. The dust was settling; there was no further gunfire.

John chaffed at his captivity. Rachael was in trouble, and he couldn't be of assistance. He moved restlessly on the springless seat. Bold Hunter stiffened, his scowl growing deeper. John stretched out, trying to see around the canopy. Jeremy was riding toward them with Rachael in the saddle in front of him.

"Into the wagon with you," Jeremy said kindly to Rachael. She slid down from her perch in front of him. Bold Hunter helped her into the wagon, almost pushing her in his effort to get her out of sight. Rachael's face had been pale. John had never seen fear in her eyes before. "My fault!" he muttered.

Jeremy rode beside John, his uniform torn and dirty. His normally symmetrical face looked lop-sided with its puffed mouth and the angry red swelling around his left eye.

"You have the makings of a beautiful black eye, Yank," John said. He figured he knew what had happened.

Jeremy's explanation came thickly from his injured mouth. "Couple of wiseacre soldiers had bold intentions. They jumped me and were keelhauling me when Rachael had the wit to signal for help. She fired my rifle. Best keep her out of sight whenever we can," he advised, running a hand through his disordered hair. His face looked sheepish. "Should have known better than to let her leave the wagon train."

John nodded, his mouth tight.

"Forgot the fish in the excitement. I'll ride back for it. By the way, I believe I'll live. Still have all my teeth. Thanks for your tender concern."

John grinned. "Yanks are tougher than army boots." He cocked his head appraisingly. "I think

I like your face better this way." He ducked Jeremy's wild swing.

Late that afternoon when they halted to make camp, the wagon train was still two miles south of Rattlesnake Springs. John stretched his tired muscles.

The children exploded from the wagon. It was empty except for Mrs. Ross. John climbed inside, seating himself beside her on the rough boards. "Good evening, madam. I just happened to be in your neighborhood, so I decided to pay a social call," he said with forced cheerfulness. Her pale skin was drawn tight across her face. Bright pink burned on her thin cheeks. "May I present my calling card?" He kissed her cheek tenderly.

"Dear, how warm you look! And handsome, too. God answered our prayer," Charity said, a wane smile lighting her face. "Rachael told me about that lovely girl. You shall bring her here so I can thank her properly." A fit of coughing forced her to lie back. John grimaced at her pillow, a half-empty sack of hominy grits.

"Naturally I'll bring the young lady if that's what you want. The new shawl is very becoming."

"Thank you, but I realize I'm not very tidy. Did you notice how lovely she is? Hope, I mean? Such beautiful hair. Her skin is as white as swan's down." She reached for John's hand. "I do desire my grandchildren to be fair-skinned."

John's voice rose in spite of himself. "Please, Mother, don't picture me as one of her suitors, kissing her fingertips in adoring reverence. She's a

162

frigid New Englander, and I've no intentions of courting her." Outside the wagon, other ears heard his declaration.

"I'll bring Miss Worchester so you can thank her, but she doesn't even like me."

"Of course she likes you. Any girl would feel it an honor to have your interest." Mrs. Ross gazed fondly into his face. John wouldn't look her in the eye.

She traced her finger down his straight nose, the patrician nose of her people. His deep blue eyes fringed with dark lashes could startle one with the intensity of his gaze. She had seen them turn almost gray when he resolved to have his will accomplished. She had also seen them flash blue sparks many times. Even she dared not face him when he was angry. She had seen them full of fun, laughter, amusement, or reckless adventure. But she had never before seen the haunting sadness which he was trying to disguise with banter. The love that shone in them now turned the deep blue almost black. She knew he was worried about her. She sighed deeply.

John looked out the rear flap, checking on Rachael's progress with the fish. "I have to find some firewood. We'll have a healthy dinner tonight, thanks to Jeremy" he said. "You rest until it is served." He folded his clean buckskin britches to make a pillow for her and then left after kissing her forehead lightly.

John searched for Jeremy. The need to be under constant guard was extremely irritating. After a futile search, John decided, "Friend Jeremy, I'll have to go without you this once." He slipped into a dense thicket of trees.

The blood surged in his veins. He was free for a few minutes. The quiet woods beckoned like a siren. John's long strides took him deep into the green solitude. The woods were crisscrossed with gurgling mountain streams, running over rocky beds singing their alluring song. Entering a small glade, he began gathering dead wood.

Even before he heard the horse, some sixth sense warned him of impending danger. The hair on the back of his neck bristled. "Only Jeremy, hot on the trail," he ferverently hoped.

Ben McDonal's big roan crashed into the arena. John dropped the wood in a heap at his feet.

"I thought I seen you tryin' to escape," Mc-Donal's voice echoed eerily. "Old Bess here'll have somepun to say about thet." He shifted the large chaw of tobacco in his mouth. Unfurling the bullwhip, he pressed his horse close to John. The whip snapped, hostile and wicked toward John. Instantly he ducked. The whip cut the air above his head.

The tip slashed the roan's flank. He jumped forward, rearing, almost unseating McDonal. With a harsh jerk, McDonal pulled the horse around, raking his spurs across the scarred sides of the plunging animal, riding straight for John. Quickly John sidestepped the flashing hooves.

McDonal wheeled his horse, cracking the whip at John. Again John dodged, but the whip cut through his sleeve, slashing his arm. John's mind was working quickly, coldly calculating the distance the bullwhip could travel. He felt no fear, but he realized the big man was getting closer each time. If he ever connected, he'd rain the blows so hard and fast that John knew he'd have no chance to recover. He had to act fast.

McDonal was coming again. John figured the risk. As the whip came snaking toward him, John caught it with his right hand. The whip cut deep into his flesh. Grimacing with pain, John hauled on the whip with all his strength. McDonal fell awkwardly from the saddle, losing his grip on the bullwhip. John whirled the whip around and around his head, then released it. With a loud whistling noise, it went sailing out of sight into the woods.

Ben got slowly to his feet, his cold gray eyes narrowed to slits, and his mouth a slash of meanness across his flushed face. A meaty hand reached to his belt and pulled out one of the new bowie knives. "I'm gonna take enough skin offen your hide to make me a new whip," he snarled, breathing loudly through his mouth in an excited hissing sound.

In the gathering dusk, John looked almost frail by comparison, his wide shoulders, compact hips, and tall figure dwarfed by the bully. Perhaps it was his Scottish blood, coming from those ancestors of his who fought with such wild fervor, but John felt a strange exhilaration now that the waiting for the inevitable had ended and the action had begun.

The excitement was heady. He was not frightened; he felt strong and confident in that knowledge.

McDonal crouched, his knife ready. John circled away. The knife glinted razor-sharp and deadly. McDonal's face looked like the devil himself.

Thank God Dad had me trained in Nagewasa or I wouldn't stand a chance against this mountain of a man, flashed through John's mind.

McDonal lunged. John pivoted. Grasping McDonal's knife hand, he slammed it hard over his knee. McDonal grunted, but held tight. John spun out of his reach.

The incredible strength of the man! If he gets a hold on me it will be the end. The absolute control of emotion necessary for this branch of jujitsu enabled John to face the man calmly, though the fever in his blood almost made him reckless.

Again the two men circled. John kept backing toward the trees. Sweat glistened on the older man's forehead. He spit his tobacco out, shut his lips firmly, and rushed. John grabbed the heavily muscled arm, then neatly flipped McDonal over his back. The huge man landed heavily.

When McDonal stood, he was limping, his breath coming in heavy pants. He stood beneath the trees, swaying his bristling head back and forth like a wounded bull. Then he rushed again. John circled warily away. Again and again McDonal tried to slash John with the knife, but he kept dodging just beyond the point. McDonal was tiring, his lunges becoming careless.

I'll wear him down, then throw him so hard he won't get up. That'll give me time to get back to the wagon train. Jeremy'll take it from there.

Another reckless lunge, and Ben was off balance. Dashing in before he could regain his footing, John grabbed his knife arm at the wrist between both hands. Following the direction of McDonal's momentum, John pulled Ben toward himself. Rolling onto his back, he kicked McDonal in the stomach with both feet; then, flipping his legs straight, he sent McDonal flying over his head. McDonal landed in a groaning heap.

John had expected Ben to be heavy, but it had taken much more effort to throw him than he had anticipated. John's legs were drained of strength. He forced himself up onto shaking legs.

He couldn't believe it! The man was up again and still had that knife in his hand! A chill of fear rippled down John's backbone. Was the man invincible? The look on his face spelled death as he thundered toward John with a burst of strength drudged up from some hidden reserve. Using the man's own strength and weight against him, John twisted McDonal's extended knife arm so that the heavy man cartwheeled through the air, landing on his chest. The heavy thud was followed by a long, low moan. Then McDonal lay where he had fallen.

John stood, legs braced apart, ready for another attack. Minutes passed. *He's tricking me. Wants me to go close enough so he can get hold of me.* He didn't take his eyes off Ben.

"What's going on here?" the voice had the unmistakable ring of authority.

One of the soldiers. John heard the clink of a sword. *An officer!* Not taking his eyes off the fallen man, John answered, "I came out here to gather firewood, sir. Ben McDonal followed me and accused me of trying to escape. He knew I wasn't, but he took the opportunity of finding me alone here to try to use a bullwhip on me. You'll find his whip over there in the trees." John pointed to where he had thrown the whip.

"Then he pulled a knife. I defended myself. He must have lost his wind when I threw him," John finished.

He faced the soldier. A lieutenant sat stiffly on his horse staring at McDonal. The shadows were now so long and deep that John couldn't make out his face beneath the cocked hat. "Private McDonal, your fun's over now," the officer said. "The army knows your fondness for 'Old Bess.' General Scott will have something to say to you."

McDonal didn't move. The officer dismounted, striding quickly to his side. He stooped over the inert body. "Someone with more authority than Scott is holding his court-martial," he declared. "He's dead. Fell on his own knife." The officer's face was solemn.

John's mind was confused. What had the lieutenant said? Then a wave of shock hit him, speeding his already racing pulse, turning his skin cold, making him shake.

The two men stared at each other.

168

"You're fortunate I arrived when I did, young man. It's obvious to me you're telling the truth, but of course there will be an inquiry. You could have been in serious trouble if the army thought you had murdered McDonal." The lieutenant's voice sounded blurred in John's ears.

"I'll have to get some men to witness the position of the body," he continued. "You'll have to reconstruct the fight. I don't see how you ever managed to best McDonal. You ride his horse back to camp. I'll be right behind you. Can you manage?" The lieutenant looked at John's white face. "I know how you feel. Felt the same way when I killed my first Indian. No offense."

John stumbled to the roan. The saddle looked higher than a saddle had ever looked before. He was so tired. Riding through the dark trees in the twilight with the officer was like a fantasy. The horse glided along, his hooves never touching the ground. The trees swayed back and forth, reaching out ghostly arms for him. A mist swirled up around him. He would wake soon and perhaps find himself back inside the stockade.

"We're here. Climb down," the lieutenant ordered. Jeremy saw John sit a minute longer in the saddle, a glazed look in his eyes. Moving in slow motion, he obediently dismounted. Jeremy came over and took John's arm, guiding him over to the campfire. He threw his own blanket over John's shoulders. Pouring a steaming tin of coffee, he placed it in John's hands. John shivered under the blanket.

The lieutenant left to make his report, telling Jeremy, "Keep him here. I'll need him later tonight."

"Break out the first aid tin, will you, Tom?" Jeremy called to a friend. Jeremy examined John's injured hand. John didn't notice; he sat staring blindly into the fire.

"Look at this. What do you suppose would make a cut like that?" Jeremy asked his friend as he prepared to clean and bind the wound. It was still bleeding and apparently had been for some time. The cut ran across the palm, cutting the web of skin between the thumb and index finger. It was about a quarter-inch wide. The small bones were exposed.

Jeremy exclaimed, "A bullwhip! Of course. He's run up against McDonal. Why does Lieutenant Whitsell want to see him again? Where is Ben McDonal?"

With the third cup of coffee, the glazed expression faded from John's eyes. His shoulders slumped. He looked near exhaustion.

Lieutenant Whitsell rode up, leading McDonal's roan to bring back the body. "Let's go, Ross. Private Worchester, I'll need you and a couple other men. Bring a horse for Ross."

Back in the glade with the flickering light from the pine torches casting deep shadows over the men, the dense darkness of the surrounding forest seemed to crowd in. This was as close to hell as John ever wanted to get.

15

"The Lord has taken you through the fires of purging more than most Christians I know," Jeremy said as John dismounted beside his wagon very late that night. "He must want you for a vessel of gold."

John smiled tiredly. "Tell me what you're talking about sometime when I'm not so trail worn." He looked at the silent wagon. "Does Mother know what happened?"

"Yep. Sent word to her that you were all right. She was not to worry." John rolled up in his blanket beside the campfire. "Thanks, Jeremy," he mumbled, asleep almost before his head touched the ground.

By the time he awoke the next morning, everyone on the wagon train knew his story. The sun was already up. A typical autumn day—blue sky, leaves brushed red and bronze, air cold and fresh. As he rolled out of the blanket, his muscles began to complain. Some of them refused to cooperate, forcing him to hobble like an old man.

The smoke curled up from the campfire, trailing overhead through the low branches of the firs, then wafting up into the bright sky. The aroma of johnnycakes and coffee hung about the camp. John wolfed breakfast.

He attempted to help Bold Hunter with the team, but he couldn't do much. His hand throbbed painfully, so he spent the time with Charity inside the wagon, rolling up the canvas on her side to allow her to enjoy the lovely morning. She had to hear the story of his struggle with McDonal from his own lips.

When the bugle blew for the wagons to roll, Bold Hunter drove. John climbed up stiffly to sit beside him. Neither mentioned the fight; they rode without exchanging a word.

Just before noon they arrived at Rattlesnake Springs, Tennessee. Here they would camp and resupply their food for the trip.

Seventeen thousand Indians were being exiled. John learned from Jeremy that there would be twelve separate wagon trains, each with approximately 1,000 to 1,500 captives, from Tennessee, Georgia, Alabama, and North and South Carolina. A regiment of infantry, a regiment of artillery, six companies of dragoons, plus 4,000 militiamen would guard the exiles.

To encourage themselves, the Indians began to liken themselves to the twelve tribes of Israel leaving the Egyptian captivity for the freedom of the promised land of milk and honey. They needed encouragement, for many were sick.

Another wagon train was already camped outside of town. In spite of the exile, John's spirits began to climb. The glorious fall day, coupled with the exciting hustle and bustle of townspeople interacting with the soldiers and militiamen, the busy campers, and the new arrivals setting up camp all combined to cheer him.

The town consisted of one long main street, fenced on both sides by unpainted wooden buildings. A wooden sidewalk stretched on both sides of the narrow dirt street. The sidewalk was crowded with people, mostly men. Military horses were hitched along the street.

"Glad to see you looking so chipper this morning," Jeremy greeted John. "You're something of a legend today."

"I'm considering changing my name to David," John joked.

"If you have any ideas of changing my name to Jonathan, forget it!" Jeremy said with a straight face.

"All tomfoolery aside, without God's protection that would have been me slung across that horse you led back to the wagon train last night," John said.

"Yep." Jeremy's wide green eyes were serious. "Think what a loss for womanhood that would have been."

"You're just jealous!" John laughed, taking a poke at Jeremy's grinning face. "The lieutenant ordered us to stay with the wagons," he said, a boyish longing was in his face. "I certainly would like to go in and see the town."

"Just the reason I'm here. Thought you might

want to sightsee for a spell. But don't get any ideas about slipping off again. Every man in my dragoon knows who you are." Jeremy lowered his voice. "You're under special guard, too."

"I've been under special guard ever since I met you," John quipped lightly. Even though he had killed a man, John had come to terms with his guilt feelings. The fight had been in self-defense. He was now free from the threat the wagon master had held over him since the day of his capture. His heart was light.

Jumping stiffly down from the wagon, John joined Jeremy on the dirt road. As they walked jauntily toward town, people they passed stopped to stare.

"Why are they eyeballing us?" Jeremy asked.

John grinned. "You're a fine-looking gentleman with that lopsided mouth and black eye. I've got my hand bandaged almost to my elbow, hobbling down the street stiff as a British soldier. We look like a couple of Jean Lafitte's pirates."

Setting his hat at a rackish angle on his head, Jeremy hooked his thumbs into his crossbelts and began to swagger. The two glared at any man who looked like he might be too timid to fight. They couldn't hold back the laughter when an old man hurriedly crossed the street to avoid them.

The town was busier than on the Fourth of July. Hogs had long since been routed from their wallows in the middle of the town's lone street. Buckboards were crowded with families in a gala mood who were gawking like country girls at the encampment of soldiers and Indians. In more elegant equipages sat the leading ladies of the county, their faces curious beneath their coal-scuttle bonnets. Beside them drove their husbands or beaux in claw-hammer coats of green or blue.

Soldiers, their blue uniforms shiny with epaulets and brass buttons, strode about importantly with many a self-conscious swipe at their side-whiskers. The doors of the town's one tavern were swinging constantly.

The town loafers sat idly in groups, whittling, spitting tobacco juice, and spinning yarns. John was for going into the tavern, but Jeremy thought it best not to.

The town was too small to hold their interest long. The array of camped wagons with the bivouac guards provided a more enticing scene. They were camped just east of town. John could see the seeming confusion really had a pattern. Wagons were parked in irregular circles almost linking them together. Beyond the circles were hobbled the oxen, and farther out, in ever-widening circles like ripples in a lake, were the cavalry horses and artillery regiments. Some of the soldiers were standing guard duty, while others wandered freely. Everywhere was the smart blue uniform with the white crossbelts of the regular army. Harder to distinguish from the Indians were the baggy trousers of the militia. Coonskin caps and muzzle-loading rifles were abundant. The flashing swords, jangling spurs, and gold braid of the officers spiced the potpourri of men.

Looking bedraggled and tacky were the Indians. Some were dressed in baggy pants or tunics with turbans on their heads looking like mystics from an Eastern land. Others were dressed in buckskin or otter. Hundreds were shivering in summer-weight homespun. A good portion of the Indians were barefoot. John winced, remembering how cold his feet had been before God provided him with shoes.

The Indians maintained their innate dignity as they moved about their wagons. Though forced to remain in camp, they were not idle. The men were fashioning blowguns from river cane to be used for small-game hunting. Others were making darts for the blowguns from locust wood, feathering them with thistledown. Some of the Indians were making knives chipped from flint with heavy rocks. John even spotted one man making a battleax, attaching a stone ball to a sycamore stripling with rawhide. No, the men were not idle, but John knew they were thinking more of food than of rebellion. They were continuing to be obedient to the voice of Chief Ross.

John appreciated the beauty of the Cherokee women even after months of imprisonment. They were tall, slender, vivacious, with graceful walk and even features, darkly lovely. The sprinkling of browns and blondes among the raven tresses revealed the mixed blood. No wonder so many soldiers found themselves lounging in the vicinity of the busy girls and women. Some of the women bent over campfires, preparing dinner, while others were weaving baskets from honeysuckle vines, white oak splints, ash splints, river cane, or whatever material they had gathered. Others dried medicinal herbs in the sun on lines made from wild hemp.

Some women were taking advantage of the camping time to fashion bowls and pots of pottery. They had dug under the topsoil for the clay, which they dried by the fire and then pulverized into powder. This they mixed with water. With their fingers they coiled strips of clay, upward from the base to the rim. Occasionally they fashioned it by setting it on a flat rock and moving it smoothly round and round. They polished the surface with a stone, then fired it.

John was proud of his people. The only things they had at their disposal were raw materials. Yet, whatever they needed, given time, they would be able to provide for themselves.

If the men were permitted to hunt, they could bring back the animal pelts to make warm clothing. But would they be permitted to hunt? Was there enough time to dry the skins, scrape them smooth, and sew them before winter? Already the days were crisp, the nights cold. Frost was in the air.

Thinking of the several hundred graves left behind in New Echota, John felt Pris's warm arms round his neck; her sweet moist kiss on his cheek. He swallowed hard. How he missed her. How many other graves would remain beside the trail to

Oklahoma if his people didn't get warm clothes before snow?

"Yank, are we sanctioned to hunt?"

"How can the army allow the Indians to go running to the forest to hunt? They could easily escape. Part of our job is to supply meat for the wagon train."

"What about the skins? Do we get the skins for clothes?"

"Couldn't say. The militia do pretty much what they want. Those pelts are worth a lot of money."

"Let's move over toward the river near the campground," John suggested.

On the banks of the river, women were busy washing clothes, carrying water, digging for clay. Scores of children played beside the clear, fast-flowing mountain stream.

Despite their captivity, the women were cheerful, although their work was hampered by the soldiers who stood underfoot watching the girls. John was glad Rachael was staying in the wagon. He had had enough trouble over her.

He dug out his pocketknife, cutting some long pieces of river cane. He chose strong, straight lengths about six feet long. He searched for and found some other items he needed. Jeremy stood nearby, his attention on the girls. When a girl noticed Jeremy watching, she lowered her head shyly, turning gracefully away.

Next John searched the rocky stream for some large pieces of flint, which he pocketed.

All he had to find now was wild hemp.

Jeremy started with a jerk, glancing hurriedly at the sun. "Ho, John, we can't idle here all day," he said urgently. "I've got to stand guard duty. Let's have a footrace back."

"I've a fancy you'd be glad to race me today," John replied lightly. "I can't run. I'm so stiff I can scarcely hobble."

"I've got to get back or I'm in trouble," Jeremy's freckled face was anxious. "Give me your word of honor you'll go back to the wagon. I'm responsible for you."

"Word of honor. Don't fret about me. I'll meander back to the wagon."

John hadn't even finished speaking before Jeremy was running hard for his post. John chuckled as he watched the redhead dodge in and out through the surging mass of people and animals, leaving startled gasps at near collisions in his wake.

John followed leisurely, deciding to detour through town. He was smiling to himself as he watched two drunken militiamen trying to help each other stand up outside the saloon, when he saw Hope. She had her back to him, but there was no mistaking that small form. He could easily circle her tiny waist with both hands. Her sunbonnet had been replaced by a perky little hat with a wisp of a veil, revealing golden red hair gleaming brightly in the sunlight. Suddenly one of the drunks stumbled against her.

With his most gentlemanly drawl, John said, "If I may be so bold as to assist you, ma'am." He

179

elbowed the drunks out of her path, then set them on their course down the street. They went on their way like two sodden canoes wallowing in a sudden gale.

"I am honored, sir." He liked that crisp New England accent. He saw with amusement the shock on her face when she looked up and recognized him.

"You shouldn't be on the street alone, Miss Worchester." John took her elbow, guiding her firmly down the street while balancing the river cane on his shoulder with his injured hand. "It will be my pleasure to see you to your wagon."

"Aren't you Mr. Ross?" She wasn't sure. How could he be walking freely in the street? Also, this man was such a gentleman.

John laughed gently at her confusion. "Yes, Miss Worchester. And very happy that I happened along at such a timely moment." His blue eyes danced with amusement.

As they walked, she seemed unaware of the stares from the soldiers, militiamen, and townspeople. *She's obviously accustomed to people looking at her,* John thought. *She's a beauty all right.* She was looking at John sideways, her dimples playing games around her lips. "I was expecting Captain Peterson," she said. "He promised to accompany me; but since you are here, I may as well let you."

As though you've got anything to say about it! John thought as he kept a firm grip on her elbow.

"Miss Worchester, my mother would be

180

pleased to have you call. She wants to thank you personally for your generous gifts." John's drawl was very polite.

"Oh, that isn't necessary. There is no need for thanks. I would be happy to meet your mother, though. Father has spoken of her often. I hope your hand is not badly injured. Like everyone else on the wagon train, I heard of your adventure."

"It's nothing, just a small cut."

"I'm so happy to hear that. I understand you and Jeremy have become good friends. At first I found that hard to believe. You appeared so fierce and angry, to say nothing of being rude. Jeremy has never made a habit of being close to crude people. I don't mean to offend, but I had rather a poor opinion of you. I can see now that I was mistaken. Forgive me."

John marveled at the incredible honesty of the girl. No girl he had ever known had been so outspoken. Obviously she still was unaware of how her brother had spent his first three years in the army.

"No need." John kept his voice casual. "We met under some rather trying circumstances. I was rude. I hope you'll forgive me."

Those green eyes that so easily prodded him to anger were making him feel a little weak inside, a strange quivering feeling. She had such large eyes, he could almost lose himself in their depths.

"Hope, wait! Here I am," an anguished voice called. The tardy Captain Peterson was rushing toward them, his black hair falling in waves over a high forehead. Eager brown eyes sought Hope's.

Before the captain could say another word, John interrupted sternly, "Captain Peterson, you left this young lady unescorted in a dangerous place. Fortunately, as a friend of the family, I came to her rescue. As you may have noticed, there is no room on the sidewalk for three. Your services are no longer necessary. You may return to your regiment."

Eagerness exploded into anger. The dark face flushed. Ignoring John, Peterson said, "I'm sorry, Hope. I got here as quickly as I could. Lieutenant Whitsell was giving his report."

"Miss Worchester has promised to pay a call to my mother. I'm escorting her to our wagon." John spoke as though the plan were already confirmed. The dark eyes of the captain looked questioningly into Hope's sparkling green ones.

"Yes, Matthew, what Mr. Ross says is true." She touched the soldier's sleeve lightly, "You may call on Father and me tonight after dinner," she invited. John wondered if she ever invited Indians.

The captain wasn't going to surrender. "Ross, what are you doing here?" For the first time he had noticed who his rival was.

"I thought I just explained that, Captain. I'm taking the lady to visit my mother," John's voice oozed patience.

"You just can't walk around town. You're a prisoner. From the report I just heard, I'd vote to put you behind bars until you get dumped in Oklahoma!'' He habitually spoke in an explosive burst of words, not unattractive, as if his virility couldn't be compressed into an even flow.

John answered coolly, "I'm under special guard, didn't they tell you?" John firmly guided Hope toward the train.

"I'm sorry Matthew," Hope said. "I really have committed myself. Please come tonight," she called over her shoulder as John hustled her away, leaving Captain Peterson glaring at them from the middle of the boardwalk.

She laughed up at John, "You're rather accustomed to getting your own way, aren't you?"

"Not recently." He could see she had enjoyed the little drama tremendously. She really was a likable person. Just now she had fallen into his scheme with the same fun her brother would have shown. He looked triumphantly back at the grim-faced captain, but an uneasy feeling prickled his neck.

As they approached John's wagon, a bright-eyed tyke, Lone Feather, danced up to John, loudly asking, "Is this the girl you said nobody was going to force you to court? Is it, John? Huh? Is it? Is this the frigid New Englander? She's—" John hand shot out, muffling the words Lone Feather was trying to say. He held the squirming child and muttered in his ear, "Not now! Go away!"

Hope's eyes flashed. "You are a crude person! I shall see your mother because I keep my word. But I never want to see *you* again. Frigid New

Englander! Let me tell you, Mr. Ross, New Englanders can be as hot in passion as they can in their loathing!'' The crisp voice was cold, distant, and ruthlessly truthful.

16

Hope climbed into the wagon without a backward look.

"Phew! There's a girl who says what she thinks. No pretense with her." John said glumly.

"Did I do something wrong?" asked Lone Feather in a subdued voice.

"Rather. I would have preferred you to have asked me privately. Go play, will you?"

John was shaken. It had been delightful becoming acquainted with Hope, but his hasty words had ruined that relationship.

Where was Rachael? Bold Hunter was missing too. John stood close to the wagon, trying not to appear to be eavesdropping. He couldn't hear a thing, just the low murmur of voices, spiced now and again with laughter. *They seem to be getting along well,"* he thought. *Why do I have so much trouble with this particular young lady? Being in her vicinity is as dangerous as being near a keg of gunpowder on the Fourth of July.* The comparison tickled him. Both were small and had to be handled with care.

John took out his pocketknife to work on his

blowgun. He searched for the straightest piece of slender hickory rod to work down inside the river cane. After the interior of the cane was clean and smooth, John feathered the yellow locust shaft with thistledown. "This hand slows me down so much that I'm as clumsy as a bear at a ball," he complained. When he finished, the evening shadows were long. Hope was still inside the wagon.

Soon Bold Hunter came with a load of dead branches which he threw onto the campfire and fired it. Then Rachael appeared and bent over the cooking pot as she started to prepare their meal. Noticing John's gloomy face, she asked, "Is your mother worse?"

"No, the Worchester girl is inside talking to her."

"Oh?" Rachael seemed surprised, but her face became impassive.

Only Bold Hunter seemed cheered by the news.

John stretched his long legs, not attempting to hide the weapons which he had made. He moved restlessly away from the wagon. In the west the wild, rugged peaks thrust up their tips, row upon row against the skyline. As the sun slid behind the mountains, gold, pink, and purple splendor splashed the sky, then faded into bronze and gray. The golds, reds, and browns of the trees darkened into cold dullness.

It must be dark inside the wagon. What is that girl doing? John wondered. *Is she planning to stay all night? If she doesn't leave soon, I'm going to*

186

take matters into my own hands. Finally the flap opened. Hope lifted her long skirts, climbing easily to the ground. Not even glancing in John's direction, she headed for the line of soldiers guarding the wagons. *She looks like she can take care of herself,* John thought as he watched her walk toward Jeremy's post. Her leaving without a word gave him the same feeling of loss he had experienced when the sunset faded into cold dusk.

After supper, John went to find Jeremy.

"What's wrong, John? You look like you lost your last friend." Jeremy was sitting close to the fire, drinking steaming coffee with a few other soldiers.

"Nothing. Do you have a Bible?" John ignored the mocking looks.

"Yep. Want to read it?" Jeremy's voice revealed his pleasure.

"Yes. Read it with me, will you? I need some help understanding it." John knew Jeremy well enough to know he would drop anything to help someone grow in his understanding of God.

They went back to John's wagon, where Rachael eagerly joined them. Sitting close to the uncertain light of the campfire, Jeremy asked, "What do you want to read?"

John smiled at Rachael. "You choose." In the flickering firelight, John felt love for these two, his brother and sister in Christ. He wished his mother were not already asleep.

"John looked a little sad at supper tonight. Read something to cheer him up," Rachael said softly.

187

Her eyes were tender when she looked at him.

John sat hunched by the fire, chin on his knees, idly tracing a picture in the dirt. "Last night you talked about 'fires of purging' and 'vessels of gold.'" he said to Jeremy. "What did you mean?"

"I think 2 Timothy, chapter two is what we want." Jeremy read the chapter slowly. Then he began to earnestly explain the parts he had in mind the night before.

"Verse 3 says to endure hardness as a good soldier of Jesus Christ. Verse 10 says we must be willing to suffer if it will bring glory to Christ Jesus." Rachel and John were sitting close together, looking expectantly at Jeremy. John reached for her hand as Jeremy continued. "Verse 12 tells us, 'If we suffer, we shall also reign with him: if we deny him, he also will deny us.' When we think that our suffering is hard, just remember that someday we shall rule and reign with Christ. But if we give up when we suffer, or turn against Christ, He also must deny us. So you need to read the Bible to get to know the very nature of God. Get to know God personally so that you can trust Him no matter what happens. *Trust* is the key, John. If you trust God, you can have faith that no matter what happens to you, He knows what is best."

Under cover of the darkness, John drew Rachael closer. He squeezed her hand. "Yes, when we trust God, we know that whatever happens to us, it's the best possible thing," Rachael said confidently. "To me, that's the greatest joy in the Christian life."

"You're saying that God makes no mistakes?" John asked.

"That's about it," Jeremy continued. "When you stop and think about it, you get a real feeling of security. Here's the part I had in mind last night: verse 20, the vessel of gold made to honor Christ. A vessel of gold is one that is purged or cleansed by fire so Christ can use you for His highest will. Any questions?"

"I thought my sin was cleansed when I accepted Christ as my Saviour," John said in a puzzled voice.

"Purging is more than cleansing. It's a strengthening of character, a removal of the flaws which culture or environment or genetics may have engraved on a personality. It's the shaping of a new personality which the Holy Spirit can use. God wants us to be conformed to the image of Christ. Purging is one way He helps us to conform."

"Does God purge nations as well as individuals?"

"Yes, God had to purge the nation of Israel time and time again. Purging always seems to include suffering in some form."

"Oh, John, you're right!" Rachael said excitedly. "I'm sure you're right. You're thinking about our Cherokee nation. God is purging our nation right now. Hundreds of our people have turned to Christ since they've lost everything else. Even the witch doctors are becoming converted."

In an anguished tone, John asked, "But why

does He allow the innocent babies to suffer? Why did my baby sister, Pris, have to die, Jeremy?"

"Perhaps God wanted to spare the child the suffering that is still ahead," Jeremy suggested softly.

Tears glistened on Rachael's cheeks as John continued, his voice breaking with emotion. "But she wanted to live, to enjoy life, to be loved and to love, to find God's plan for her life, to experience the beauty of creation. Now she's gone. Why was she born, if only to die so soon? Why is there so much emptiness without her?"

Jeremy had to steady his own voice. "I'm not sure I have all the answers."

"I *need* some answers!" John blurted out. "I can't just blindly accept events with no logical explanation, and then say I trust God. How can a merciful, just God allow the innocent to suffer?" John's voice rose with his agitation. Unconsciously he gripped Rachael's hand so hard that she was forced to pull it away.

"As far as Pris is concerned, you said she wanted to experience love and life to their fullest," Jeremy said quietly. "I believe that's exactly what she is doing now. She has entered the place of absolute love. She is with God, who *is* love. How much more fully can one experience love? As far as experiencing life is concerned, Jesus said, 'I am come that they might have life, and that they might have it more abundantly.'* If Jesus brings the abundant life to us here on earth, it stands to

*John 10:10

190

reason that life in heaven must be truly abundant above all that we could ever dream of."

John stared into the flickering flames. Jeremy was right of course. It eased the pain in his heart, but unanswered questions still churned in his head. Sin was at the bottom of suffering, whether always directly or sometimes indirectly. Suffering was necessary in the plan of God. God's plan to make a member of a spoiled species into a member of His holy family necessitated a radical reforming of the species. It made him weary to think of the job God had on His hands.

"Let me borrow your Bible will you, Yank? I can read it during the day, and then we can study together at night."

"I was hoping you'd ask. Keep my Bible for a while, but I'll need it now and again. I've got needs of my own."

After Jeremy left, Rachael said, "You're a very tender person beneath that strong exterior. I like that in a man." She disappeared inside the wagon before he could answer.

John threw more wood on the fire, wrapped his blanket around his long body, and then stretched out near the heat. But sleep wouldn't come. He moved restlessly on the hard ground as he reviewed over and over in his mind the night's discussion. The blanket was too short, the air too cold. Close to the fire it was too hot; farther away it was too cold. At best, one side was uncomfortably warm while the other was cold.

From somewhere up high near the mountaintop,

a wildcat screamed. The chilling sound brought a new flow of thoughts, a strategy to escape in order to go hunting. He had to bring in meat and skins, and it would have to be soon because the wagon train would leave Rattlesnake Springs before long. At least his weapons were ready.

John lay on his back looking up into the velvet darkness. A mellow harvest moon shone brilliantly, casting deep shadows in the woods. The wagons stood clearly outlined in the valley, but deep shadows lay behind them. Good cover. Hundreds of campfires dotted the area. Shadowy forms lay surrounding each one. A deep hush filled the valley.

A rustling, soft but unnatural, made John turn. At first he could see nothing. Bold Hunter was at his elbow before he saw him in the shadows. In a barely audible whisper, he spoke in John's ear, "Bold Hunter go hunting, too. Go at dawn?"

"Two will be missed. No, I go alone."

Bold Hunter shook his head stubbornly. "You no stop Bold Hunter."

John sighed. "When the guard changes, they talk. Put the wagon between them and us. Head toward the river."

Midnight came, heralded by the cry of a mountain owl. The deep, wild, lonely cry roused a need, an aching, a desire in his body. He felt himself tense, his flesh tingling. He tried to divert his thinking, but thoughts of Rachael were mixed with thoughts of Hope.

In desperation John prayed. Confessing his

need for help, he laid his problem before the Lord. His tension began to leave and his body relax, calming his passion.

He dozed until the song of a cardinal high in a balsam tree woke him. In the darkness John folded his blanket and then crawled silently away from the dead fire. With the wagon between himself and the guard, he looked over the clearing to the forest, feeling rather than hearing Bold Hunter slip up beside him. Each had a blowgun and several darts.

"I'll go first. If I make it, I'll wait for you beneath those trees," John whispered.

The first faint light of dawn began to filter over the mountains. They watched without breathing as the new guard appeared. The two guards greeted each other, resting their gun butts on the ground. John could see their breath, frosty in the morning light. He slid from shadow to shadow until he was back of the next wagon. His heart was pounding. Straining his eyes for a guard posted in an unexpected spot, he moved silently and swiftly from cover to cover. Finally he stood in the trees. Nearby a horse whinnied. Then Bold Hunter joined him.

They ran swiftly toward the rushing stream. Reaching it, they followed it upward toward the mountains into the denser woods.

The sun rose in a burst of color, and birds chirped a greeting to the day. Behind them a distant bugle blew. Dew was heavy on the grass. The stream was crystal clear, rushing down over the rugged rocks. They ran along its banks until they could no longer hear the muted noise from camp.

It was exhilarating to run in the early morning chill, to experience his muscles pumping, and to feel the crisp air in his lungs. They passed a waterfall shot through with diamonds from shafts of sunlight filtering through the trees.

How sweet the taste of freedom! Why should one man have the power to hold another prisoner? Wasn't there room on earth for all men to be free?

They ran with the grace and power of panthers. When they were winded, they hid near a deepening of the stream and then waited.

The sounds of the forest were a symphony. The calm beauty penetrated John's heart, relaxing his nerves. The sun shone warm on his head and shoulders. Chipmunks and squirrels came to drink. As John leaned comfortably against a tree, his eyelids became heavy. It was hard to keep awake after having had so little sleep last night. He began to drowse.

A flash of red alerted him; the red fox must have smelled them.

John smelled the unforgettable fragrance of autumn, of dying things. Still, it was a season he loved. A slight breeze rustled the brightly colored leaves above his head, and they drifted down into dead mounds on the mossy ground. Back at New Echota, the faded autumn leaves would be falling on the newly mounded graves. Would the memory always be so painful?

John's thoughts turned toward the Lord. Belatedly, he wondered if the Lord wanted him

194

where he was. Maybe he shouldn't have come. "Lord, bless us with game," he prayed. "Forgive us if we shouldn't have come. But You know that the children need meat and warm clothes."

A buck stole to the water's edge. Raising his delicate muzzle to the air, he sniffed. Under his breath Bold Hunter repeated the charm a Cherokee hunter must say before aiming at an animal. He asked the buck's permission to kill it.

Raising their blowguns, both of them aimed, then blew. The slight puff of wind or whine of the dart alerted the animal. At the crucial instant the deer moved. John's dart fell short, but Bold Hunter's penetrated the buck's front shoulder. Quicker than thought, the buck wheeled, heading for denser woods. Both young men raced after him.

John was glad the deer had chosen to run toward the wagon encampment rather than on up the mountain. It wouldn't be so far to carry it. They fought their way through the dense underbrush, low-hanging branches catching at their clothes. The deer was faltering. They slipped and slid on the slippery moss, often jumping the ironlike bushes that obstructed their path. A misstep could send them hurtling down a steep gully.

Floundering through a heavy growth of rhododendron, the hunters stumbled upon the fallen deer. He lay on his side, panting heavily. Large brown eyes stared, wide with fright and pain.

"He's mine!" cried Bold Hunter, whipping out

his knife. Quickly he put the wounded animal out of its pain.

Suddenly the hair on the back of John's neck bristled, a sixth sense warning him of danger. With a loud, spine-chilling screech, a wildcat, ears laid flat against his head and fur bristling, leaped down from an overhead limb, landing squarely on Bold Hunter's back.

The young men had not been the only hunters.

17

For a stunned split second John stood immobile, the wildcat's blood-chilling scream ringing in his ears. Heedless of the danger—his only thought was of Bold Hunter pinned helpless beneath the heavy cat's clawing, biting fury—John leaped onto the wildcat's back.

Wrapping his long legs around the animal's body while hooking one arm around the pulsating neck and the other around a foreleg, John tore the wildcat free, then rolled him off Bold Hunter's back. Pinned beneath the furious animal, John hung onto him as tightly as possible. The cat screeched and clawed at the air, repeatedly turning his head and showing his yellowed teeth as he tried to bite John. *Can't hold him long,* John thought with panic as his hold began weakening.

Eyes wide with fright, Bold Hunter pushed himself to his knees. Slashing the exposed cat's belly with his knife, he received three long scratches down the outside of his arm in return. The animal's screech ended in an almost humanlike scream of pain. His paws jerked, then his head lolled to one side. The round yellow eyes stared unblinking at the sun as he died.

Pushing off the dead weight, John lay on the ground, too weak to stand. Bold Hunter stared down at him, his right sleeve torn off and blood dripping down his arm. *We were lucky,* John thought. *No, it wasn't luck. If Bold Hunter had been unconscious or if he had lost his knife when that cat jumped him, I'd have gotten mauled, maybe even killed. I couldn't have held that cat another thirty seconds, if that long.*

When Bold Hunter recovered his breath, his voice held a note of disbelief. "Why you save Bold Hunter's life?"

"All I thought of when that cat landed was that you were going to die. I couldn't just stand there," John answered, his voice more unsteady than he would have liked. He sat up. "Let's see your back."

Bold Hunter turned. John expected to see the young Indian's back slashed in ribbons, but instead, there were two rather deep claw marks on his shoulders where the cat's front feet had landed, and lighter impressions left by the rear feet. The wounds were bleeding feeely. The wildcat had torn off a hunk of Bold Hunter's hair, trying to get at his neck.

Under Bold Hunter's direction, John gathered herbs and then bound them tightly over the wounds with wild grapevine. As John worked, the Indian began to talk.

"Shaman witch doctor make strong medicine for Bold Hunter. Strong medicine for hunt. Medicine no work. Make strong medicine for love.

198

Love medicine no work. Rachael no marry. Bold Hunter see God of white man stronger than witch doctor." He sat unflinching as John bound his wounds.

"Bold Hunter say Christian scared," he continued. "Bold Hunter wrong. Bold Hunter hear you strong in fight with wagon master, see you strong in love, and see you strong in saving life of Bold Hunter. You no scared."

John shrugged. "I can't say I wasn't scared."

"You no have weapon to fight wildcat, but you fight. You think you God help?"

"I didn't have much chance to think!"

Bold Hunter cleaned his knife on the grass. Skillfully he began to skin the wildcat. "Find young sapling to tie deer on," he said. "We carry back to wagon."

When John returned carrying the sapling, Bold Hunter had the wildcat pelt neatly bundled. They tied the deer's front and rear feet to the sapling with grapevines. Then, with a determined look in his eye, the dark young man stood and faced the light young man. "Bold Hunter ready to take God of white man," he declared.

John was stunned. He stared at Bold Hunter. *Is he ribbing me?* he wondered. "That's fine," he finally managed.

Bold Hunter looked at him with impatience. Obviously he expected John to do something.

"You mean *now?*" John questioned in amazement. Bold Hunter nodded.

John wiped nervous hands on his legs. He

hardly knew what to say. He didn't want to say the wrong thing. "Just tell God what you want to do, then ask the Lord Jesus to come into your life and forgive your sins," John's voice trailed off. He hated to remind Bold Hunter of his sins; perhaps that would turn him away.

But without hesitation the Indian dropped to his knees and raised his arms toward heaven. In a loud, strong voice he prayed as he looked toward the brilliant blue sky, "O God of John Ross, Bold Hunter want Lord Jesus come into life. Bold Hunter want all evil forgiven. Bold Hunter say yes to God of white man. Want God become God of Bold Hunter."

Then the young Indian began to speak rapidly in Cherokee. John felt awed as he watched the strongly muscled man unashamedly pour his heart out to God. The large black eyes were no longer burning with hatred or contempt, for the tender shine of worship lighted them as God poured out His Holy Spirit upon him.

John blinked hard against a softness he didn't want Bold Hunter to see. When he had finished praying, Bold Hunter stood and placed both hands on John's shoulders and gazed deep into his blue eyes. No barrier of hatred stood between them now. "Ross lift heart of Bold Hunter when heart flat," he said, "From where sun now stand, we brothers."

Bold Hunter slung the wildcat skin over John's shoulder, then took the sapling supporting the front legs of the deer. John took the other end of the sapling. Carrying the deer between them supported on the pole, the hunters returned to the wagon train.

As they trudged through the dense undergrowth, Bold Hunter suddenly stopped short. "Wait!" he commanded. He put down his load and disappeared among the trees.

When he returned a few minutes later, he carried a white eagle feather. "John Ross wear sacred eagle feather of Cherokee brave proudly. You earn." He attached the feather to a lock of John's hair, letting it hang down the back, Cherokee fashion.

The late afternoon sun was casting long shadows when the two approached Rattlesnake Springs.

"How we get in camp?" Bold Hunter asked. "Wait till dark? Maybe guards not miss?"

"Oh, we've been missed; there's no doubt about that. Look, there are four soldiers on duty around our wagon." John's heart lurched, wondering if Rachael were all right. "No, we will walk in like free men. There aren't many soldiers off duty down there, so they must be in the woods searching for us. If they've been doing double duty all day looking for us, they will be mighty resentful. We had best go face the wrath of the army."

"Pray first," Bold Hunter said.

John felt embarrassed. Why hadn't he thought of that? They bowed their heads, and the young Indian waited for John to pray.

"Father, give the authorities understanding

201

that we were only trying to help our people. We pray that the punishment might be light. In Jesus' name. Amen."

With the deer swinging gently between them, they strode into the clearing and headed toward the wagons. The off-duty soldiers gaped with mouths hanging open. When no one attempted to stop them, John felt a surge of hope.

But when they entered the Indian encampment, they were the immediate center of attention. Indian women and children, old men and young, rose to their feet. The sight of free men returning home from a successful hunt swept the area like a refreshing wind. The self-image of the captive people rose on that wind. New vitality radiated from the faces of the Indians as the people began to chant the century-old "Song of the Successful Hunt." The words rose and fell, growing louder as the hunters neared their own wagon.

John hadn't even considered what their appearance would signify to the captive Indians. All around them, men and boys reached for their own homemade weapons. Waving them wildly above their heads, they chanted words he couldn't understand.

Never had John felt more atune to his people. As a boy he had dreamed of a similar hunt and the welcome home, but he had never had much hope of its fulfillment.

Suddenly a large detachment of armed soldiers broke through the crowd. "Break it up! Break it up!" they shouted. But their efforts to quell the

Indians had no effect. The crowd became wilder, the chanting louder. John and Bold Hunter were surrounded by the armed guard, young soldiers who looked frightened.

"Go back to your wagons and quiet down!" The order was repeated over and over. Finally more armed soldiers arrived and made the Indians return to their wagons. But as they went they held their weapons high, and the triumphant chant continued.

John could see that the soldiers feared revolt. Being unable to speak the Cherokee language, the army did not have the slightest idea that the Indians were merely performing a vigorous ceremonial welcome.

Their game was seized. Prodded by numerous guns, John and Bold Hunter were ordered to raise their hands and march to the commanding officer's tent.

As they marched the length of the camp, the chanting followed them. Quick as a whisper from one person to another, the chanting kept pace with the marchers. It was like one candle lighting another until a great bonfire raged. The nervous soldiers had their guns primed, cocked with fingers on the triggers.

Worry began gnawing at the corners of John's mind. What kind of wild thing had developed? Matters had certainly gotten out of hand. He was convinced that Bold Hunter and he would have to pay for starting this commotion. He prayed that nobody would get trigger-happy.

Then John spotted Jeremy. Ruefully he grinned. Jeremy looked him square in the eye. His face was closed, his mouth tight-lipped, his eyes showed no friendliness.

John's grin faded and his heart began to pound faster. He could feel his temples pulsing furiously and his body beginning to sag with weariness. *I must be in real trouble for Jeremy to be so angry,* he thought.

They were nearing the lead wagon when John realized that they would soon march past the Worchester wagon. "God, please don't let her see me," he prayed fervently.

But there Hope was, sitting on her horse with an excellent view of the whole parade. John felt his face burning. Even his ears got hot. He set his jaw. His devil-may-care disguise was not too convincing, topped as it was with a flaming face. For a second their eyes met across the excited mob of Indians. Her expression was unreadable. As he continued to stare, she lifted her small chin and pink spots began to burn in her cheeks. She turned away.

She's still angry. A confused hurt pierced his heart. *"Why did You let this misunderstanding happen, Lord?"* he asked silently.

By now John's arms felt so heavy that he lowered them slightly. Immediately several bayonets prodded painfully into his flesh. "Keep those hands high!" a harsh voice ordered.

Ten minutes later, the two young Christians were facing the commanding officer, General Win-

204

field Scott. John had heard the soldier's nickname, for Scott was "Old Fuss and Feathers."

His headquarters were immaculate. They stood waiting a few minutes for the general to appear. On his table lay several thick volumes, a trimmed kerosene lamp, quill and ink, and an orderly pile of maps as well as a stack of parchment paper. Everything was squarely in place. The general was obviously a man who permitted no disorder or lack of discipline in either himself or his men. John felt a bit awed. The general was a national war hero, a man of courage. During the last war, Scott had had two horses shot from under him at Lundy's Lane. He had distinguished himself as perhaps the top field general the United States had ever produced. He was a strategical genius.

Two orderlies snapped to attention as Scott entered the room with all the ceremony of a state dinner. Upon his entrance, the plain tent assumed a formal atmosphere. A sense of hopelessness crept over John when he saw the general's stern uncompromising face. The man's mouth was thin, drawn down at the corners, giving him an expression of perpetual disgust. A hawklike nose protruded beneath a pair of sharply penetrating eyes. Every man entering the tent was in full-dress uniform. Guards stood at attention on either side of the canvas door.

Outside, the chanting stopped. John could hear his heart beating loudly in the silence. General Scott sat stiffly behind the table, looking steadily at the two captives. His voice was unexpectedly kind. "Were you two the cause of this tumult?"

"Yes, sir," John answered.

"Names?"

They gave their names. John noticed a stenographer was recording everything.

"Are you related to Chief Ross?" General Scott demanded.

"Yes, sir. He's my uncle."

"You two have caused considerable problems for the United States Army today. Half a regiment had to take double duty to search the woods for you. Somehow you activated the Indians into a rebellious mob. If you had not been recaptured, your actions would have incited many more Indians to attempt escape. This is a serious offense. The punishment for escaped Indians who are caught is the firing squad."

18

John's world lurched. The firing squad! His knees went weak and sweat beaded his forehead. He looked sideways at Bold Hunter, standing straight and tall, a calm half-smile on his lips. John could almost read his mind.

He's ready to die. He's not afraid, because he's a Christian now. But I'm not ready to go right now! John's thoughts screamed in his head. *Too many things left unfinished. I want to live for the Lord.*

The general had been talking. What was he saying? With an effort John forced his attention back to General Scott.

Scott's voice was impatient. "I repeat, do you have anything to say in your defense?"

"Yes, sir," John answered. He swallowed, then cleared his throat nervously. Trying hard to keep his voice steady, he began. "We have sixteen children in our wagon. All of their parents died in the smallpox epidemic inside the prison at New Echota." John's voice caught on the lump in his throat. "My baby sister died there too."

He coughed, trying to clear the lump from his throat. His voice was getting more emotional than he wanted. Why couldn't he make it calm, impersonal? "The children are barefoot, wearing torn summer clothes. They're cold, hungry, and some are sick. We have had no fresh meat." John leaned forward, forgetting himself as he described the children.

"The children have become thin, their bodies weakened because they have not received enough to eat. They whimper at night inside the wagon when the temperature falls and the cold winds blow. Soon the snow will come. If the children do not get warm clothes and more food, they will die."

John's intense blue eyes were begging the general to do something for the children. John clenched his fists. Unconsciously taking a step toward the general, he went on passionately, "Over 200 silent graves mark the beginning of our exile. If something is not done, the trail from here to Oklahoma will be remembered by future generations as a trail of death."

General Scott didn't move. Except for the slow crimson flush that began beneath the rigid collar of his uniform and crawled inexorably toward his hairline, he seemed unmoved.

"These things pressed so heavily on me that I decided to provide my wagon with fresh meat and pelts for warm clothes." John straightened, a challenging light gleaming in his eyes. "We did not try to escape, and we weren't captured. We returned to camp freely, walking in from the forest with our game tied between us. Our one desire was to provide for our people"

Scott's thin lips barely moved as he spiked the question, "And the riot?"

John's answer was quick and sure. "Hope. My people have been free for countless generations. We are a proud, self-reliant, self-governing people, unused to captivity. My people are depressed and unhappy. Some have lost their desire to live since they have lost their homes and families. Seeing two of their own people returning as of old from the hunt kindled a flicker of hope in their hearts. That hope flamed higher as they innocently and quite naturally began to chant the Cherokee 'Song of the Successful Hunt.' The people were drawn together in a bond of hope for the future. The soldiers didn't understand. They thought the happy chanting was the beginning of a riot."

Scott sat, his bushy brows knit together in a dark frown. Minutes passed. John began to feel very tired. He had done his best, but would it change anything? The room was taut with expectancy. John became aware of the pain in his hand, the weariness in his body, the emptiness in his stomach. Would the trial never end?

"You knew you would be punished when you returned to camp, did you not?"

"Yes, sir."

General Scott leaned back in his chair. He folded his arms across his chest. "Did it ever occur to you that my soldiers might provide your wagon with meat?"

"Yes, sir. I asked one of your men if the army

would provide the pelts as well as the meat. He answered that the army might, but the militia probably would not. We've been on the wagon train several weeks now, and during that time I've not seen any fresh meat or pelts provided.''

"What was the soldier's name?" barked Scott.

"I'd rather not say, sir."

Scott tapped his desk with the end of his quill. He pursed his mouth, frowning. John began to think he was going to have to stand in front of those penetrating eyes forever. He stiffened his knees, trying to hide his fatigue.

"I believe your defense. There will be no firing squad. However, leaving camp without a guard calls for strong disciplinary measures. On the other hand, your motives were good. Tempering mercy with justice is the American way, though you as a Cherokee may find that difficult to believe. Your sentence is a week's discipline under Captain Peterson, who will, I believe, instill in you both a high regard for obedience to the army. At night you shall be handcuffed to the wagon."

John didn't realize he had been holding his breath until he released it in relief. "Thank you, sir," he said gratefully.

"Orderly, take these two to the medic; then release them to Peterson," the general commanded. From the tone of voice he used, Scott had already dismissed them from his mind.

Two guards followed Bold Hunter and John into the roomy hospital tent where a slender man dressed in rumpled trousers and an army shirt sat

210

writing at a long table. In the glow from the hanging kerosene lamp, his strong features stood in sharp relief on his thin face. John could only estimate his age as somewhere between forty and sixty. His high intelligent forehead was heavily furrowed, his head sparsely covered with thin sandy hair. Apparently he took little notice of the way he dressed, but the tent was spotless.

Two cots made up with snowy linen stood along one end of the tent. Books packed neatly in a carton, their dust covers conveniently in view, were within easy reach of the doctor's folding chair. Surgical tools, arranged neatly in rows on another table near one of the cots, were also covered with white linen. Bottles and beakers, carefully packed in crates, sat at the end of another table. On the same table a chess set was ready. The tent had the atmosphere of clean efficiency plus homey comfort.

Curious eyes welcomed them. "You guards may wait outside. Tell my aide to get you some coffee," the medic said, dismissing the guards.

A warm smile lighted the thin face, making it look years younger. John began to relax. "So you're the two who caused all the excitement today." He nodded to John. "You look tired. Sit down on the cot while I examine your friend."

He made a careful examination of Bold Hunter's wounds. After he had cleaned and medicated them, he replaced the medicinal herbs on the deepest gashes and bound them with white bandages. "I don't think these will slow you up any," he commented. Bold Hunter started to put his shirt back on, but the doctor stopped him. "While you're here, I want to give you a thorough check-up. I'm doing research on the effect of captivity on the human body." When he had finished examining Bold Hunter, the doctor looked a bit puzzled. "You're about the finest specimen of manhood I've ever seen. I can't see where being a prisoner has had any adverse effect on you." Bold Hunter looked impassive. John began to understand that that was Bold Hunter's cover when he became embarrassed.

The doctor turned to John. "Your turn."

"I'm not injured."

"Let's take a look at that hand while you're here."

After unwrapping the dirty bandage, the medic whistled softly as he looked at John's injured hand. The wound was still open, raw and painful-looking. Small bones gleamed whitely through yellow pus, and streaks of red ran up John's wrist. John felt a little sick.

"You've got a nice little infection here. I'm going to have to clean this out, then sew you up," the doctor said casually. "We're going to have to get that blood poisoning stopped, or you'll lose your hand."

Methodically choosing his instruments, he took several bottles from the crate and then poured a solution into a large pan. With slow movements reminding John of a great musician, the doctor selected a large needle.

212

As he walked toward John, the large needle ready in his hand, the color drained out of John's face and his eyes closed. The medic caught him as he slumped to the floor. "Help me ease him onto the cot," he said to Bold Hunter. After they had settled John on the cot in the position the doctor wanted, he commented, "The needle distresses the best of them! Strange, seems it's usually the big blades that faint when they see this instrument." He looked at his needle lovingly, much as a horse breeder might look at his favorite broodmare.

When John fainted, Bold Hunter's mouth dropped in amazement. He thought John was strong in love and in war and in anything else he might have to face.

"Better this way; it's a painful job," the doctor muttered as he lanced the hand skillfully, forcing out the pus. When he began the delicate job of stitching the raw flesh of John's palm together, Bold Hunter's face took on a greenish tinge as he watched. Soon he turned his head.

"Get that blanket off that other cot and cover Ross," the doctor ordered. When the doctor had completed his mending, he placed John's limp hand to soak in the chemical solution. Then he took another bottle from the neatly packed crate. Slipping to his knees beside the cot, he poured some of the liquid into John's mouth. John choked, coughed, and swallowed. His eyelids fluttered open.

"Ow, my hand! What did you do to it?" He tried

213

to struggle up, pulling his hand out of the pan. The doctor pushed him down none too gently and forced his hand back into the solution.

"Lie still and take it easy. It's all over but the soaking. Your hand will be painful for a couple of weeks, but it should be as good as new after that. Did a beautiful job, even though I must say so myself."

John lay back against the hard pillow, an embarrassed look on his pale face. *I must have fainted,* he thought, *probably because we haven't eaten all day.* He felt relief that the operation was over.

"We'll have some grub for you boys in a few shakes," the doctor said, as if he had read John's mind. "Hope you don't mind army rations."

"Sounds good to me," John answered. "I could eat a dog about now."

The doctor looked at him as though he thought all Indians ate dogs anyway. John was too tired to bother to straighten him out.

He dozed until the aide brought in supper. The doctor, although used to soldiers with hearty appetites, was amazed at the amount of food the two young men stowed away.

After supper John leaned back in his folding chair and let out his belt a notch. He grinned with satisfaction as he reached for a third cup of coffee.

"That hand surely didn't slow down your eating any," the doctor commented. "You put more away with just your left hand than most men do with both hands." He chuckled as he leaned back in his chair and filled a pipe. The scent of tobacco filled the tent as he lit a match and puffed his pipe into life. "Bold Hunter, you can leave anytime," he said. "But I'm going to keep you here a while, Ross. Got to get rid of that blood poisoning. I want to keep close tabs on you until that's gone. We'll be hitting the trail tomorrow, so you'll have to ride in the medical wagon with me."

John rubbed his eyes wearily. With a yawn he asked Bold Hunter, "Would you bring me Jeremy's Bible? I left it folded in my blanket under the wagon."

"Glad to bring God's Word to brother." The words seemed to loosen Bold Hunter's silent tongue, for he then told the doctor how John had saved his life. John propped his head on his good hand, trying to keep his heavy eyes open while Bold Hunter talked. Openly, without embarrassment, Bold Hunter related how he had accepted the white man's God as his God because of the way John lived.

The doctor seemed interested. He let his pipe grow cold as he was caught up in the story, and his twinkling gray eyes became serious. Periodically he nodded, encouraging Bold Hunter to go on. "So, you end up here. I'd say you fellows are pretty lucky to be alive."

It was dark when Bold Hunter left the tent, but John saw one of the guards leave with him. The other stayed by the hospital tent door.

"Take your shirt off, Ross. I want to look you over," the doctor ordered. He ran his hands over the scars on John's back, making no other com-

215

ment than "Must have been some herbal healing used here. Looks pretty good." Evidently he had come across some of the other Indians who had been whipped. He took his time, examining John closely. "I've got some medication that'll help the dysentery. Better take the medication now," he went on. "You should have told me about it before we ate. You've got some congestion in your lungs, too, so you'll have to take it easy until I can get you back on your feet." He gave John some foul-tasting medicine to choke down.

"How is it you've lost so much weight when your friend is in such good shape?" he asked.

John shrugged his shoulders. He didn't feel like telling this man about sharing his food with the hungry children, research or no research.

"Strange that Bold Hunter didn't get dysentery. That would account for some of the weight. Was he overweight when he was captured?"

"He's lost some weight," John replied. "I think he was accustomed to a stoic way of life. He ate and slept outdoors a good bit anyway. Maybe he built up more immunity to disease that way."

"How about you? What kind of life did you have?"

John looked at the cot, wishing that the doctor would hurry and complete his examination. "Pretty much like yours, I presume," he said tiredly. He missed the doctor's look of amazement.

The doctor settled John on the extra cot, putting his hand in the solution to soak again. He was sleeping soundly when the doctor removed his hand and bandaged it. The doctor sat silently, looking at John a long time before he blew out the lantern.

19

The next morning the doctor let John sleep. He and his aides worked quietly around his sleeping form until the medical wagon was loaded. Then he woke John, fed him a hearty breakfast, and soaked his hand.

Bold Hunter strode into the tent. "Here Jeremy's Bible."

"Much obliged. How's Mother?" John asked.

"Not good." Seeing the pained look on John's face, Bold Hunter said, "Rachael take good care of Mrs. Ross." Unable to contain his delight, Bold Hunter added happily, "Rachael glad Bold Hunter Christian." John had been thinking how delighted Rachael would be to find Bold Hunter had become a Christian. With a sinking feeling, he wondered just how glad she was.

"Bold Hunter go now. Learn to obey soldiers." The last was said with a significant shrug of his shoulder and a wink of one of his dark shining eyes.

"Who's driving our wagon?" John called after Bold Hunter's retreating back.

"Small redhead drive until Bold Hunter get

back. He keep soldiers away from Rachael. I trust.''

John was relieved. *Even if Jeremy is upset with me, he's still a good friend,* he thought.

The doctor came in just after Bold Hunter left. "I see your friend is about to learn obedience."

"So the law dictated! Sir, do you have medicine for a bad cough?"

"Depends. Is there a fever?"

"Yes, my mother's pretty flushed. She doesn't have much appetite."

"How long has she been this way?"

"At least a week."

"Sounds like I ought to take a look at her."

"She's in the last wagon. I'm pretty worried about her."

The doctor looked at John suspiciously. "This isn't a trick so that you can escape is it?"

"No, sir, on my word of honor it isn't."

The doctor searched John's face, then decided to take a chance.

"Let me bandage that hand first, and we're on our way."

The aide was packing the last of the tent poles into the wagon as they left. The doctor carried his black medical bag, and John noticed that the guard who had been posted at the hospital tent was following them closely. As they walked back toward the end of the wagon train, it began to move west. Wagon after wagon slowly lumbered across the valley floor.

Passing one wagon, they both saw a small Indian

219

girl poke her head out the end of the wagon and vomit. The doctor made a mental note.

"Them younguns sure like to puke. They do that all day long," a disgusted soldier's voice complained.

John's old anger blazed, "Dolt! You drag these children away from their homes and then don't give them enough to eat! If they're sick and hungry it's your fault!" The anger in his voice made the soldier step back. "Why don't you quit complaining and try calling the doctor when you see they are ill?"

As John walked over to the child, the soldier asked in an undertone, "Hey, Doc, who is he?"

The doctor spoke loud enough for John to hear. "Chief's nephew. Better do as he says, or you'll be on the carpet."

After they passed, John asked, "Were you ridiculing me, sir?"

"No. These soldiers know Ross is in charge of the train under General Scott. Doesn't hurt to spread your name around, son."

"Hm. Maybe that's why we didn't get much in the way of punishment," John mused.

"You're wrong there. General Scott is a just man. He wouldn't care if you were his own nephew. In fact, if you had been, you would have been given a stiffer sentence. Don't go thinking you got off so light. Army discipline is rough on men who have difficulty obeying orders. Captain Peterson's got free rein to do just about anything he wants with you if you disobey. You'd better decide right now to do everything he says fast and well. Never talk back; just 'Yes, sir; right away, sir.' I notice you aren't afraid to say what you think. Better learn to keep your mouth shut.''

John decided to start praying now about the week of discipline. "I wish it were under anybody else," he said. "Peterson's certain to be nursing a grudge."

"He'll work your tail off. I've decided not to release you from the hospital until your hand's well. You can't do much with it the way it is now."

"I'm grateful to you for that, sir. That was worrying me. It still aches intensely."

John spotted Jeremy's red head driving the Ross wagon. "There it is," he told the doctor. "The last wagon, enveloped in the dust. The girl beside the soldier is Rachael Whiteswan. I hope he's behaving himself," John joked.

"Well, son, you are traveling in purty company. Is that your girl or your friend's?"

"That's what I'd like to know."

Jeremy stopped the wagon and helped the doctor climb in. He picked up the reins to go on without speaking to John. Rachael beamed her welcome. "You've not broken the chain," she said sweetly. At his blank look she explained, "First Reverend Worchester introduced you to Christ, then you initiated Bold Hunter, and now it's his turn to forge a golden link of love."

"That's a delightful way of expressing it." John grinned up at Jeremy. "Hello, Yank. Hold up a minute. I need to talk to you," he said anxiously.

"I'll drive while you and Jeremy talk," Rachael offered, taking the reins from Jeremy.

"Thanks, Rachael." John's look conveyed more than thanks.

As Jeremy jumped down to walk beside John, his unfriendly face revealed a cold, controlled anger. He had been deeply hurt.

"Give me a chance to explain!" John pleaded with him. "I couldn't tell you I planned to go hunting. You'd have stopped me or you would have had to report me. Believe me, I wanted to tell you; you're the best friend I have. Don't be angry."

Jeremy's face relaxed slightly.

"It must have been God's will that we go, since Bold Hunter became a Christian," John continued. "I had to go and get some fresh meat for these hungry children. But I knew you'd stop me because it was your duty."

"Apology accepted. But it'll be a long time before I trust you out of my sight again, you Southern chevalier. You put me through a turbulent time. When you disappeared, I was accused of helping you escape. Scott had me at headquarters for a couple hours questioning me. It was only by the grace of God I was able to take over the wagon while you and Bold Hunter serve your sentences. Those two Georgia legioners who jumped me earlier, trying to get Rachael, wanted to drive the wagon."

"Are you absolutely certain that you don't want

to change your name to Jonathan?" John asked, his heart feeling a good bit lighter.

Jeremy took a swing at him. "Ho, how'd you draw Peterson as your discipline?"

"Pure good fortune! Did you mention his name to General Scott?"

"Nope. Why should I? He's a friend of Hope's, you know."

"I know," John answered ruefully. "I sent him on his way like a bad little boy when he was late meeting your sister in Rattlesnake Springs. He didn't relish being treated that way," he finished, unhappiness obvious in his tone of voice.

Jeremy looked surprised. "Was that the time she came storming into camp demanding that Peterson take her back to the wagon?"

"That was the time I offended her totally without intention."

Jeremy threw back his head, laughing heartily. John didn't think it was so funny.

"So, you're like all the soldiers in the regiment. You like my sister. Isn't Rachael enough for you? Do you have to have all the pretty girls?"

"Your sting is worse than a nettle!" John's voice sounded grumpier than he had intended.

"Ha! If Peterson knows you are interested in Hope, he's going to ride you every time he gets a chance. He wants to marry her. She just keeps him dangling."

"She's not in love with him?"

"She's not found a man yet with love enough to

hold her. Take my advice and stay away from her."

"That should be easy. She has an exceedingly low opinion of me. What kind of discipline is Peterson devising?"

"Bold Hunter's busy grooming the horses, shining the artillery, drilling, and keeping Peterson's coffee cup filled. Nothing too bad. Same thing we do every day, except for the drilling. We've gotten plenty of that during garrison duty."

The doctor's head appeared at the opening in the front of the wagon. "I'm ready."

"Thank's for everything, Yank. Take good care of Rachael for us."

"Yep. Read that Bible all you can. You won't get time for it next week."

John and the doctor walked toward the hospital wagon.

"How is she, sir?"

"I left some medicine for a couple of the children." The doctor answered, his voice solemn.

"Yes, sir, but what about Mother?"

"Son, there's nothing I can do for her. She's dying."

The words slipped into John's consciousness like shadows, then flamed into painful crimson capitals. "SHE'S DYING!" The burning letters shot like jagged spears into each particle of his brain until he thought his head would explode. "I have to go back to stay with her, sir."

"I've been ordered not to release you to Wor-

224

chester's custody. I'll arrange for another guard,"
the doctor replied.

"That soldier following us has been guarding me
ever since we left the hospital wagon. Can't you
release me to his custody?"

"Right. I'll send the solution. Soak your hand at
least six times a day until the red streaks disap-
pear. Report to me—uh—when it's over. I'm
sorry."

Charity's face became pink with pleasure when
John slipped into the wagon to sit beside her. He
tenderly took her in his arms, trying to shield her
from the bumps caused by the wagon lurching on
the rutty road. Resting her head against his broad
chest, she breathed a sigh of deep contentment.
He stroked her hair. "Rachael told me all that
happened," she said. "I couldn't be prouder."

He whispered in her ear, "I love you, Mother.
No man could ever have asked for a better
mother."

Her voice was so soft that he had to strain to
hear it. "I'm glad you know, dear. I'm ready to
go." John couldn't speak. Hot tears pricked behind his eyelids.

The children sitting silently in the wagon recognized the look of death. They had seen it on their
own mothers' faces back in the stockade. Respect-
fully, they looked away, allowing mother and son
this last time together. They had grown to love
Mrs. Ross, so her dying was an agonizing repeat of
the loss they felt when their own mothers had died.

Tears washed clean streaks down many dirty faces.

"Carry on the generation of Ross, and bring honor to your name, my son," Mrs. Ross said. "Promise me to serve God all your life."

"As long as the mountains last, as long as the sun shines, as long as the rivers flow, I promise to serve God," John vowed, using the sacred Cherokee pledge for the first time in his life. He felt as though his heart was being torn into fragments. He couldn't stand the pain much longer, but she needed him.

"Don't become bitter, dear. I'm happy."

"I'll do my best."

The sun was casting feeble rays in the west, failing in its last attempt to overcome the gray clouds when Charity said, soft as a breath, "Look, John, how bright it has become. The light is dazzling!"

John saw no bright light, only his mother's face. The years fell away, making her look as bright and eager as a young girl on her wedding day.

"Oh, my beautiful Saviour! I'm coming." Her voice was soft, clear, and musical, a bell tolling across the abyss between life and death. Then she was gone.

John clutched his mother, desperately wanting to bring her back. Her face, looking young and full of peace, lay against his empty heart. A tightly closed door in his mind broke open, revealing his father's face, forever frozen into a look of perpetual surprise. How irrevocable the decision he had made.

John heard the children crying and felt he should do something for them. But, instead, he sat staring stonily into the gathering darkness, as though what he saw frightened him.

The wagon had stopped and was empty when John realized he was still holding his mother's body. He laid the motionless form gently back against the half-empty bag of hominy. Anger flashed through him. His mother dying in the back of an old wagon. What a death for a McCormac! But the anger faded quickly. *This is not the end,* he realized. *For Mother, it is the beginning. I've never seen her look so happy. I could not wish her back. But Dad*—John broke off his thought, deliberately trying to forget the knowledge that haunted him.

Tenderly he wrapped his blanket around his mother's slight body and carried it toward the woods. Jeremy followed, carrying a shovel. Rachael hurried to find Reverend Worchester.

In the gloomy dusk John walked to a spot in the woods. At the base of an ancient oak, beside a bubbling stream, he began to dig. But the ground was hard and his right hand was useless. Jeremy took the shovel. The sound of the shovel digging deep into the cold earth grated John's nerves raw. The moon began to rise, casting dark shadows on the ivy-covered ground. In the uncertain light of the moon, the ivy hanging from the trees looked like dark, ghostly fingers pointing to the sky. *Why hadn't his father found the way?*

Finally Jeremy laid down the shovel and raised his arms to receive the body. Moving mechanically like a man in a dream, John gave it to him. He groaned when the first clods of dirt struck her. Another unmarked grave beside the "Trail of Tears."

Softly, her lovely alto voice hushed in reverence, Rachael began to sing a hymn. John heard her voice rise and fall, but he couldn't seem to grasp the meaning. He saw only the beauty that had been his mother crushed beneath four feet of dirt.

Pastor Worchester prayed, his sad face heavy with weariness.

The grating sound of the shovel echoed in John's ears long after he reported to Doctor Smith. A deep depression settled over him. He tried to shake it, but day after day dragged wearily by with no relief. He went through the motions of life, but there was no meaning.

Doctor Smith tried everything to revive John, but he seemed unable to respond. He ate because the doctor urged him. Then he followed the doctor listlessly on his rounds.

Toward the end of the week, the two sat warming themselves at the campfire, their backs toward the inky blackness of the night. Doctor Smith, seeking to rouse John, asked, "Where's that Bible you borrowed from the soldier with the hair red as a rusted gun barrel? I haven't seen you read it yet."

"It's in the wagon somewhere," John answered, not caring.

"Thought you planned to read it often."

"Haven't felt like it."

The fire flickered and crackled in the frosty air. John sat with his head hunched and his chin resting on his knees. The doctor rummaged in the wagon a few minutes, then returned with the Bible and a lighted lantern. Opening the Book, he turned the pages with an unfamiliar hand.

He fumbled with the book, not knowing what to do with it now that he had it. He read aloud a passage here and there. The words were strange; the people mentioned belonged to a different time and culture. Just as he had always suspected, the Bible didn't mean anything in this modern day. It was old-fashioned, outmoded. Why did people bother to read it? He was almost at the end. One more passage, then he would put it back in the wagon. He began reading aloud again.

> And God shall wipe away all tears from their eyes; and there shall be no more death, neither sorrow, nor crying, neither shall there be any more pain: for the former things are passed away. And he that sat upon the throne said, Behold, I make all things new. . . . I will give unto him that is athirst of the fountain of the water of life freely. He that overcometh shall inherit all things; and I will be his God, and he shall be my son (Revelation 21:4-7).

John's posture didn't change; he didn't stir. He didn't say a word, but his mental attitude shifted drastically. The door he had closed in his mind against God had been opened. The gentle, loving Holy Spirit began His work of filling the void in John's life with the love of God.

I've been a fool not to read the Bible when I needed it the most, John realized. That night he slept without the tossing and moaning the doctor had been so concerned with. The next day the wagon train passed through Murfreesboro, Tennessee. The change that had come over John was so remarkable that Doctor Smith's curiosity was aroused. He decided that one day he would do research on the effect of the Bible on depression.

John's appetite improved so much that the doctor had a hard time keeping him supplied with enough food. John spent much of the remaining days, when he was not busy helping the doctor, settled in the back of the wagon, reading Jeremy's Bible.

One afternoon the doctor sat down in the wagon beside John. "You play chess?" he asked.

"Yes, sir, but I haven't played for a long time. I'm pretty rusty." John closed his Bible, looking with interest at the board Doctor Smith had opened.

The time passed quickly in the rattling wagon. "Checkmate!" John announced triumphantly.

"I quit, boy! That's the third game you've won in succession. That's enough for me. I'll play you sometime when you're not so rusty."

John stretched out his long frame, then moved over to the front flap, looking out. The day was cold, skies overcast, with gray clouds hanging over the mountains. He caught sight of Captain Peterson striding toward the wagon, looking dashing with his cocked hat and long blue surtout.

Peterson stopped the wagon, motioning it to the side of the road. "Came to check on your patient, Doctor," Peterson said in a businesslike voice. "Will he be fit for duty tomorrow morning?"

"Want to take a look?" the doctor answered.

Peterson hooked his thumbs in his pistol belt and frowned. "Make it snappy." He brushed his long, black side-whiskers which the wind had blown.

Doctor Smith carefully unwrapped John's injured hand. "Needs another week, I'm afraid."

Peterson inspected John's hand, then spoke in a flat expressionless voice, "You're the doctor. I'll take charge of the prisoner one week from today." His tall, polished boots clomped loudly as he walked briskly toward his waiting squad.

"That's one disappointed man, Ross. Appears he's looking forward to getting his hands on you. What's he got a burr under his saddle for?" Doctor Smith asked curiously.

"I was indiscreet; I made a fool of him in front of a certain young lady."

"Girls like you, do they? Thought they would. Tall, handsome lad like you." He chuckled.

"*Some* girls."

The doctor smiled to himself, thinking of young

love and his own past. They climbed back into the wagon. John was glad he could stay with the doctor another week. The kindly companionship and the adequate food and rest were just what he needed. But he missed Jeremy. He hadn't seen him since his mother died. He knew that his friend drove the Ross wagon all day and then stood guard duty in the evening.

When John felt the wagon slow, he stuck his head out the front flap to find out why. A small boy of about seven, dressed in broadcloth, frantically waved them to a stop. On closer inspection, the boy's clothes proved to be well worn; his stock was torn, his shoes were full of holes. His chestnut brown hair blew back from his shoulders in the wind. "Doctor, my mother is having a baby! Please come and help her." The boy was shivering with fright or cold.

"Come, John, bring my bag." The young boy led the two men to his mother's wagon. As the doctor climbed in, John handed up the bag and looked around to see what he could do.

In a moment the doctor opened the flap. Smiling broadly, he handed a small girl down. "Here, watch her until I'm finished."

She was about three. Frightened hazel eyes stared at John. Chestnut hair hung in ringlets about her small face. The fine blue muslin dress gave no protection from the cold. "Are you the doctor?"

"No, little one. I'm just here to help him. The doctor's inside with your mommy. What's your

232

name?" He opened his shirt and pulled it around her.

She smiled, her eyes losing their fearful look as she began to charm John. "My name's Beth. I like you."

John cuddled the fragile child and told her funny stories until her sad, wistful face crinkled in amusement. It took so little to make her smile happily. His heart ached. How like Pris she was.

The boy joined them, manfully trying to hide his shivers. He wanted to laugh too. They sat in the scant protection of a large boulder, both children soon sitting snugly on John's lap. A long time passed, during which John heard an occasional moan come from inside the wagon. The children had become heavy. John's muscles were stiff but he wouldn't disturb them; they had both fallen asleep.

Much later, Doctor Smith called. The boy woke, silent and watchful. John handed the sleeping Beth in to the doctor.

"Come in and see the mother and her new son," Doctor Smith told him. "Bringing a new life into the world is one of the most rewarding things in this profession."

John climbed over the tailgate. A young woman was lying on the floor, covered with an army blanket. Her chestnut hair cascaded in damp waves around the pale oval of her face. Tired hazel eyes were underlined heavily by dark smudges, and tears clung to long, dark lashes. John felt like an intruder.

"I've never seen such a tiny baby. He's pretty. He's even got hair, fuzzy dark hair." John felt awed. He'd been around death plenty lately. It was good to be in the presence of a new life, a promise of the future.

In a hoarse whisper, the mother said, "His name is Bryce, after his father. I wish Daddy could see you, Bryce."

"Mr. Hancock was in Nashville on business when his family was taken to the stockade," the doctor explained. "They haven't seen him since."

"Bryce didn't even know we were going to have another baby. I planned to tell him when he got back."

"Who's going to take care of you and the children?" John asked, leaning toward the young woman, a worried frown on his face.

"Send Teddy for my cousin Martha. She lost all her children in the smallpox epidemic." Her delicate face was anxious as she looked at her children.

While his hand was healing in the days that followed, John learned a good bit about medicine as he assisted the doctor. Despite their best efforts, an average of four to five persons died each day. The tragic sight of a wagon pulled to the side of the dirt road to bury its dead was now a regular occurrence. The Indians began to call the westward journey the "Trail of Tears."

On the morning of his last day with Doctor Smith, John rose reluctantly. A pale November sun filtered through the oak's leafless limbs as a

234

cold wind blew from the west. The Indians called the west wind "black," the wind of death.

Doctor Smith needed John to assist him. They had to bury the gentle Mrs. Hancock and the week-old infant Bryce. Pneumonia had closed both their lungs.

What had happened to the promise of life? Would anyone survive the trip to the new territory? John laid the baby's slender body in the open grave, tenderly stroking the fuzzy head before placing it against the mother's breast. The small boy stood against the wind, his arm circled protectingly around his young sister. Bitter tears fell as another grave marked the "Trail of Tears."

If the children survived, they would always remember this place with a shudder. The remainder of the day—when he was free—John searched the Bible, his heart heavy with sorrow.

From an anguished heart, he prayed, "I can't understand all this suffering and death, Lord. All I know is that You are perfect love. You love my people more than I. Since You are allowing this tragedy to happen, I can only trust You. Your ways are right."

20

Immediately following officers' muster, Captain Peterson, the bright yellow plume on his shako waving briskly in the air, came for John.

A weak sun, topping the tall pines, sparkled on the heavy dew, turning the wagon camp into a mystical, magical scene. The heavy scent of freshly fallen pine needles filled the air.

John stood near the wagon savoring the fresh coolness of the morning as he sipped his last cup of hot coffee. He felt better than he had since becoming a prisoner. Catching sight of Peterson, John thought, *Here comes the Falcon now.*

Peterson did look like a falcon—slender, tense with suppressed ambition, his dark, piercing eyes dominating a face kept from being handsome by the hawklike nose set above thin lips.

John spoke from where he stood beside the shadowy wheel of the wagon, his soft, slow drawl catching Peterson by surprise. "Looking for me?"

Peterson's voice sounded harsh in the Georgian's ears. "Where's Doctor Smith? You're to be released to my custody this morning. I haven't time to wait." He repeatedly slapped his riding crop into his gloved hand impatiently.

"The doctor's out on a call. He released me last night before he left. He thought he might be gone all night. He—"

"Released you last night!" Peterson broke in, his voice sharp and annoyed. "Leaving you unguarded? Of all the stupid, incompetent, presumptuous fools! This will end up on his service record!" He tapped the riding crop against his leg, piercing black eyes probing John critically. "Are you fit to work?"

"My hand's pretty well healed, if that's what you mean," John drawled.

"Ross, when you address an officer, your comment shall be 'Yes, sir' unless more is required. For all practical purposes, you are now a private in the United States Army." Peterson stood as tall as he could, but he still had to tip his head back to look into John's eyes. "Your job is instant obedience of all orders. Any disobedience will be severely punished. Do you understand?" Peterson's voice was condescending, as though he were speaking to a slow-learning child.

"Yes, sir." Already John felt that the promise of a beautiful morning had been deceptive.

"Attention!" snapped Captain Peterson.

John tried. He felt foolish standing rigidly erect because of another man's desire. Around him members of the wagon train were breaking camp. Horses were being saddled, oxen hitched, fires put out, soldiers going about their duties, their voices laughing, talking, and cursing while he had to stand there looking silly.

237

"Suck in that gut!" Peterson drove his fist hard into John's solar plexus. "Keep that chin down; stand erect! You look like a wilted pansy."

John grunted, gasping for air while still attempting to stand at attention.

"Keep those heels together and eyes front," ordered Peterson in his first easy lesson on becoming a soldier.

"I shall outline your duties once. Any slip up, and you'll stand double duty like any other enlisted man. Report to my tent at 5:30 each morning for your day's orders. After serving my breakfast, you will pack my gear, load my tent, feed and saddle my horse, feed and hitch both teams to the supply wagon, and be instructed in close order drill for a specified time. During the journey you will be available to work with the teams or the wagons as necessary in fording rivers, ascending mountains, etc. In the meantime, artillery guns are to be cleaned and polished, teams hauling the guns groomed, water barrels kept full, my saddle oiled and polished, my white gloves cleaned, and my uniform brushed. My boots will be oiled and polished nightly. You report to me on the hour, every hour, regardless of my whereabouts. When the wagons halt, you are responsible for pitching my tent, unpacking my gear, and serving my supper. After supper you report to the mess hall for cleanup duty. At 8:30 P.M. report for final instructions. I do not tolerate nonpunctuality."

John groaned inwardly. Did the Falcon think that he was a Morgan horse to get all that done in

238

one day? Peterson was no gentleman taking advantage of his power this way.

Peterson sauntered over to the coffeepot suspended from the ramrod over the doctor's campfire and helped himself. Out of the corner of his eye, John watched the captain stare morosely into the fire, sipping his coffee. A group of children playing a game darted near.

Peterson started so violently that he almost spilled the steaming liquid.

He's as nervous as a den of wildcats, John thought. *The Falcon's caught, dangling helplessly on the whim of a woman. I almost feel sorry for him.*

Doctor Smith's aide had the area cleared and the wagon ready to roll before Peterson addressed John again.

"About face, march!"

John's cramped muscles were slow to respond to the message from his brain. With untrained steps he followed Peterson's marching orders. To say he felt strange marching alone down the mountainside was to put it mildly. John began to realize how much pride he had as Peterson trampled it under his polished boots.

It was with a flaming face that John, closely followed by Peterson, approached the captain's bivouac area. *I should have known,* John thought, feeling a headache coming on, *he's camped right beside the Worchester wagon.*

Peterson's voice was unnecessarily loud as he ordered, "Halt!" Keeping his eyes focused

239

straight ahead, John could feel a pair of eyes from the wagon scrutinizing them. He felt very vulnerable.

Peterson left him standing at attention, like a robot without his master, for ten minutes while he puttered around inside the tent. John's face turned from red to white to red again, but Hope didn't come out of the wagon.

Finally Peterson yelled, "Fall out!"

Guessing that he was free to get to work, John rushed inside the tent. It was much larger than the pup tents used by the regular soldiers. It contained a single cot, a table with a whale-oil lamp, and a folding chair. A wash pitcher and bowl stood on a large chest containing the captain's clothes. Peterson's toilet accessories, along with a straight razor, brush, and strap were laid out neatly on a sturdy table. A small mirror was attached to the tent pole.

Moving fast, John packed the man's personal items in his chest, stripped the cot, and then went to find the supply wagon. There it was, parked near the rear of the tent, clearly marked with the U.S. Army insignia. The other tents were already packed into wagons ready to roll. *He deliberately kept me standing at attention so I couldn't possibly get done in time,* John realized. He quickly folded the cot and the chair, taking them in one arm and the chest in the other to load on the wagon. He found it already full of barrels, boxes, crates, pup tents, and various other provisions.

Having emptied the tent, John was jerking on the poles when the bugle blew.

Working at top speed, he hitched the two teams of oxen, not stopping to feed them. Despite the chill air, sweat began to roll down his back. The driver stood by, not offering to help. Obviously he had his orders.

The wagon train was rolling, a gap widening between it and him. The Worchester wagon, a strange soldier at the reins, waited for Peterson's wagon to fall in. When John finished, the supply wagon was only minutes late.

John shivered, the sweat on his body cooled by the chill wind. That must be Peterson's horse standing alone under the willow. Where was the saddle? It had to be in the supply wagon!

John raced after the moving wagon and jumped aboard. Looking around in the dim light at the piles of goods, John spotted an English saddle half buried under pup tents. He dug it out and whistled. "Our captain must be a man of means to have a saddle like this!" Fortunately, the blanket and bridle were close. John heaved the saddle over his shoulder, took the bridle and blanket in his hands, and jumped out of the moving wagon. Whether he miscalculated slightly in his hurry or the saddle threw him off balance, he didn't know, but he fell, sprawling on the road right under the nose of the left front ox pulling the Worchester wagon. The saddle landed on his back.

The ox looked him in the eye, undoubtedly surprised. Glancing up from his ridiculous position,

John saw Hope. She was laughing. Scrambling off the road on all fours, the ludicrousness of how he must look hit John; his laughter floated on the breeze to the wagon. "I look like a saddled jackass," he laughed.

"Ross!"

Peterson's sharp voice pierced John's laughter like a knife cutting cornbread.

"You won't be laughing this afternoon when you do two extra hours of drill for not having my horse ready."

John sprang to his feet, sprinted to the horse, saddled him, and led him to the captain before he could think of more penalties.

Peterson looked handsome in the saddle. He sat easily on the horse as it pranced and pawed spiritedly in the cool morning air. John wondered if he would ever own another horse.

"Attention!" Peterson commanded.

Not this again! John thought dismally as he snapped into the hated posture.

A company of soldiers assembled by the road waiting orders from their captain. The men stood at ease while Peterson briefed them. Before dismissing them, he ordered John, "Front and center!"

John walked over to face Peterson. "These men are soldiers," he said to John. "They are men trained and disciplined in instant obedience. This training is important. An instant's hesitation in obeying an order in battle could result in death for the soldier or for the entire company.

242

"Men, this miserable half-breed Indian has one week to become a soldier." He spoke with derision. Laughter boomed from the ranks.

"He won't even know how to stand at attention," a surly voice cracked.

"Oh, I don't think you give him enough credit. Even a 'breed can learn that in a week. He might have a little trouble with 'right face and left face,' though; that's a little more complicated." Again Peterson's voice was condescending.

"They don't make Indians like they used to," a voice jeered. "Used to be when they wore that feather in their hairlock they was someone to be scared of. Nobody in their right mind would be scared of this un."

"Army training is tough," Peterson continued. Then, as though he had suddenly had an idea, he said gloatingly, "I think a wager is in order. Is there a man here who would like to put some money on Ross? I'll bet any man here that Ross doesn't make the grade. My money says he'll break under the stress of a soldier's life. Who'll take me up?" When no one offered to bet on John, Peterson doubled John's feeling of humiliation. "Ten to one. What? No one willing to take those odds?" "I'll oblige you and lose some money on the Indian," a defiant young regular said suddenly, accepting the offer. "Been saving this Gold Eagle. Ten to one is too good to pass up."

John stood rigid, his jaw muscles working involuntarily in his taut face.

"From now until noon you will be drilled in the

correct way of marching and saluting," the captain continued. "From noon until 2:00 P.M. you will fulfill your two-hour penalty drill. You will carry this rifle," he said as he tossed an ancient musket, minus the flintlock, at John, "plus a full pack." He nodded toward a sixty-pound pack lying in the dirt near the horse's dancing hoofs.

"I'll bet he won't even make it until 2:00 o'clock," a rough voice called.

"Dismissed." Peterson wheeled his horse smartly, then galloped off to the wagon train, leaving John standing in the swirling dust. The company marched after Peterson, singing.

John sagged, a doleful expression on his face. One remaining soldier, a gnarled private chewing the dead end of an old cigar, swaggered over. He pointed to the pack and said, "Let's get started." John struggled into the heavy pack.

The drill instructor put John through one of the most grueling mornings he had ever spent. While John learned to march, salute, and handle the musket acceptably, the pack rubbed his shoulders raw and the marching rubbed blisters on his feet. The ribbing Peterson had subjected him to roused John's determination to prove the man wrong.

When the sun was at its zenith, the drill instructor shared dried venison from his saddlebag. They washed it down with tepid water from his canteen.

The extra two hours of drill was almost more than John could endure. But he did. Finally the drill instructor hopped aboard his horse. John began to think of the private as "Grasshopper."

He and Bold Hunter would laugh together when he described the bowlegged old-timer. Bold Hunter had undoubtedly had the same drill instructor.

"You'll have to shanks' mare it down to the train. Cain't be more'n two-three miles down the road." Grasshopper spurred his pony to a canter. John jogged beside him, very glad to be going *down* the mountain. The pack banged against his raw shoulders.

About 2:30 P.M. a tired, dusty John reported to Captain Peterson. The captain looked grimly happy. "You failed to report in six times today, Ross. That entitles you to six consecutive nights of guard duty—midnight to dawn."

Anger boiled up within John at the unfairness of Peterson. "Lord, see me through this," he prayed fervently, trying to hide his anger. He didn't want Peterson to have the satisfaction of seeing it.

The captain immediately put John through his newly learned paces. He was disappointed to find John had become somewhat adept at marching.

"You have until 4:00 o'clock free time," Peterson stated, his voice showing his annoyance.

"Request permission for a swim, sir," John said, trying to keep his voice from sounding eager.

Peterson raised his eyebrows. Swimming in the icy water in November?

"Granted. Wilcox, don't let him out of your sight."

The fat private waddled slowly after John in the direction of the river. On the way, John slipped aboard the supply wagon and helped himself to a fresh bar of soap.

The forest oozed serenity here by the swiftly moving stream. John felt his tense, aching body begin to relax as he strolled along its bank until he found an area dammed by beavers. John looked at it with satisfaction, estimating that the water must be about six feet deep. They were far enough from the wagon train so that only a murmur of noise disturbed the therapy of the wilderness.

With much grunting and wallowing, Wilcox settled himself comfortably in the sun where he could watch. John was amused to see that the heavy round-faced man carried a tiny Chihuahua dog in a pouch slung under his left arm. A tiny ratlike face peeped at John as he undressed.

Wilcox possessed a high squeaky voice which contrasted strangely to his bulky body. "This dog is a purebred," he announced, his voice shrill with pride. "No mixed blood in him."

John ignored the slur, saying pleasantly, "What's its name?"

"Her name is Dutchess. She's from a royal family so we had to name her proper, didn't we, Dutchess? She comes from Mexico. I paid a lot of money for her when I was down there last year. We ain't never separated, is we, Dutchess?

"You really going to get *in* that water?" Wilcox asked, his soft body quivering at the thought.

"Shall I order Lieutenant Deaus to draw my water, heat it, and bring it to my tent?" John asked lightly, picking up the soap.

He plunged into the icy water, his body tingling with the cold. Swimming fast with powerful strokes, he felt the fatigue, embarrassment, and anger wash off with the dust.

While he dressed John looked with amusement at his guard. The stillness and the heat from the pale sun, combined with an overabundant lunch, had lulled the paunchy private into a sound slumber. *Why did Peterson send this fat, careless guard?* John wondered. *Does he want me to make a run for it? He can't really think seriously of me as a rival.*

The tiny dog had crawled out of her pouch and was sniffing the bushes a few feet from Wilcox's relaxed foot. When he had finished dressing, John sat down a few yards from his guard.

He felt greatly refreshed. Overhead the cardinals were singing on the top branch of a towering fir. Beside him, the rippling water, rushing toward the lowland in its rocky bed, sang a song of sadness. John's eyes rested on the faded autumn colors beneath the trees. The meadowlark warbled her song, wild and sweet and lonely. Through the leafless branches John looked longingly at the hazy hills. His throat constricted. "I'll miss these mountains," he said softly to himself. "I've seen them every day of my life. They're strong, beautiful, eternal. Whenever I look at them I get a feeling of reassurance that life will turn out all right as long as mountains last. Eternity will only have begun when the mountains are no more. Mom and Pris—"

John was brought from his musing by the yipping of the dog. It was coming from somewhere behind the trees.

"That dog's going to get herself into trouble with the wild animals if she strays too far." Wilcox continued snoring peacefully, his fat cheek pillowed on his rifle.

Springing up, John followed the Chihuahua into the thicket. *I'm making more noise than a bunch of pigs in a cornfield,* he thought ruefully, looking down at his brogues. He listened for the dog's yip. Just when he'd begun to suspect that he'd lost the animal, a series of yips led him deeper into the woods.

John froze. *Is that a voice?* he wondered. Walking stealthily, he peeked behind a large boulder blocking his path. John burst out laughing.

Miss Hope Worchester was hopping frantically on one foot, chasing the tiny brown dog. Her red hair hung in disarray down her back. She had her green skirts lifted, exposing snowy white pantaloons, in her attempt to catch the dog. One small foot was shoeless. The mischievous dog gripped a small high-topped shoe in her mouth. The shoe was bigger than the dog, but Duchess was quick enough to elude Hope's grasp, dragging the shoe out of reach.

Hearing John laugh, Hope dropped her skirts. A pink blush rose in her cheeks, but she smiled. She didn't seem surprised to see him. "Won't you please stop laughing long enough to help me get my

248

shoe from that pesky animal?'' she asked, revealing a deep dimple in each pink cheek.

John assumed a gallant pose, with one hand on his heart, and the other arm raised to the sky. ''Sir Galahad Ross to the rescue, ma'am,'' he said and then went crashing into the bushes after the dog. She was harder to corner than a rat, but John finally backed her against a large oak. After rescuing the lady's shoe, he walked sedately toward Hope.

''What are you doing out here alone, Miss Worchester?'' he asked curiously. She held out her hand for the shoe, but he shook his head.

John wore a thoughtful look, assuming the part of a detective. ''Hm, here are the facts. The lady left the wagon train, came to a secluded part of the woods, and removed her shoes. The question is, why? Did she come to meet her lover?'' The pink in Hope's cheeks deepened to scarlet. ''But why did she take off her shoes? Was she spying on someone? But who—''

''I'm afraid it's none of your business, sir,'' she broke in before he could go on. Obviously she was not about to tell him why she was there.

''If the lady wants her shoe, she is going to have to confess,'' John taunted.

''Oh, you! You're worse than the dog! I might have known you couldn't be a gentleman!'' Hope was smiling, her green eyes sparkling with fun.

''Give me my shoe!'' she commanded, regal as a queen.

John had meant to give it to her, but that was the wrong thing to say. He grinned at her delightful mimic of royalty. It was nice not to have her laughing at him for a change. He felt like laughing at her a little.

"Come and get it," he teased.

Accepting his challenge, she jumped, then lunged, and finally grabbed for the shoe, her tinkling laugh egging him on. Her head only reached to his shoulder, so John easily held the shoe out of her reach.

"You're the most impossible person I ever met!" she said, her sparkling eyes and dimples belying her words. Once again she lunged against John, trying to get her shoe.

Suddenly John thought of Peterson trying to bait him to escape because of this girl. He also thought of the gruesome week ahead when he would be under Peterson's authority. The captain was obviously going to do all he could to make it unendurable because of Hope. Maybe he'd just even the score a little with Peterson. His eyes must have warned her because she tried to step away from him, but she was too late.

He captured her in his arms. She struggled wildly. Stroking the ringlets nestling on the back of her slender white neck, he kissed her tenderly. At first she pushed away, but then her lips began to respond, urging him on. John didn't expect the fierce response he felt to the warmth and softness of her. His kiss became demanding. Abruptly he released her, his heart was beating wildly. His

250

breath was **coming faster**, so he didn't say anything. He didn't **want her** to know how much **the** kiss had affected him.

Hope looked so inviting, her eyes wide **with** excitement, her lips slightly parted. He forced himself away. Keeping his expression nonchalant, as though he kissed a girl like that every day, **he** took her hand, firmly placed her shoe in it, **then** turned on his heel and strode back toward **the** river.

As soon as he was out of her sight, he slowed his pace, wiping the perspiration from his forehead. Then the realization hit him in the pit of his stomach like a physical blow. He cared a great deal about Miss Hope Worchester. He leaned weakly against the nearest tree.

21

Lying like a sow in the sun, Wilcox was snoring loudly, his wayward dog curled innocently at his feet, when John drifted back. Deliberately choosing a spot where Wilcox couldn't easily spot him, John settled comfortably against a fallen log. He reached inside his shirt for Jeremy's Bible.

He frowned intently at the Book a few minutes before tossing it onto a pile of fallen leaves. *Face it, Ross, you've got yourself into a dilemma this time,* he thought. For a long time he sat sprawled against the tree, unmoving. Sometimes a slight smile played on his lips; more often, his face was darkly melancholy.

Duchess yapped at a sound only she could hear. Wilcox woke with a grunt. Lumbering awkwardly to his feet, his high squeaky voice sounding scared, Wilcox yelled, "Ross, where are you? I'll wring your neck like Sunday's chicken if you've run away."

John drawled, "Right behind you, Private. Hope you enjoyed your beauty sleep." The innocence in his voice angered Wilcox.

"Don't you go lying that I was sleeping on duty.

I knew where you was all the time. Just shut your mouth and march. It's time we reported in."

Precisely at 4:00 P.M. John was standing rigidly at attention before Captain Peterson.

"Take care of my horse; he's winded. I just made the fastest trip back into Nashville that this army will ever see," Peterson boasted. The captain's face was flushed. He paced impatiently up and down the road until John had completed his task. "Set up camp immediately. I've an important engagement this evening," he barked.

Pitching the large tent was an exasperating task. John was disheveled and sweaty when he finished. His fowl mood was heightened by Peterson who stood impatiently tapping his riding crop against a dirty boot, scowling at John's clumsiness.

This was only the beginning.

"Fetch hot water for my bath. This lady deserves the whole treatment." Peterson opened his clothing chest and began selecting the assorted clothes he planned to wear. He whistled happily.

John hauled buckets of cold water the three or four hundred yards from the river to the tent, heated them, and poured them into the tin bathtub. He hoped Peterson would scald himself.

While the captain soaped himself and sang in the hot water, John brushed his uniform and then started to work on the boots. He was looking for the polish when a tiny box inside the chest caught his attention. John slipped off the lid. Lying against dark blue velvet was an elegantly cut diamond ring.

How John yearned to stuff that ring down Peterson's throat! Instead, he replaced the lid, then closed the chest. Picking up the polish, he rubbed the boot with unbridled violence, his face growing angrier with each vicious swipe.

Pretending not to notice, Peterson hummed happily while he carefully trimmed his military-style black moustache. After putting an edge on his straight razor, he carefully scraped his face. "You Indians should take more care about your appearance," he commented. "With a haircut, you wouldn't look so much like a wild donkey."

John polished his thumb with the wild jab he gave the boot.

Sniffing four bottles of after-shave lotion, Peterson chose his favorite and then motioned for John to bring his clean shirt and uniform.

"I won't be here for mess." Peterson made no attempt to hide the triumph in his voice. "You eat early, then help with KP." He carefully combed his wavy hair. "No, I think that directly after you eat I'll handcuff you to the wagon. I expect to be back quite late, so I'd better attend to that before I leave."

That was good news. No cleanup tonight.

"You have ten minutes to eat. Meet me at the supply wagon exactly at 5:00 o'clock. Oh, before you leave, dump that bath water."

John threw the boots to the ground so violently that Peterson looked at him with amusement.

"Where's your bedroll?" Peterson snapped when they met at the supply wagon.

254

"I don't have one, sir."

"What happened to it?"

John was silent. He would not tell Peterson he had buried his mother in his bedroll.

Looking slightly annoyed, Peterson snapped, "Sullen Indians. That attitude will avail you nothing. If you have no bedroll, that's no concern of mine." He wrapped his greatcoat closer to ward off the chill wind.

"Get inside the wagon. There must be something in there to sleep under."

John climbed inside, glad to be out of the sharp wind. Peterson dropped inside, searching for something. He located an iron coupling in the tailgate. A businesslike snap, and John was handcuffed to the wagon. Peterson tossed two empty gunnysacks over him.

John sneezed as the flour dust sprayed him.

Peterson strode confidently over the frost-covered ground toward the Worchester wagon, the tiny box hidden under his ruffled shirt.

As John's anger ebbed, his tired body began to relax. It was awkward lying there with his hand manacled halfway up the tailgate. Awkward but not painful. Not yet, anyway.

"John, where are you?" hissed a voice through the darkness.

John straightened, scraping his elbow against the rough boards. "Up here, inside the wagon."

Jeremy vaulted inside. "How's it going? Peterson's over at the wagon making calf eyes at Hope."

"Glad you came."

"Peterson give you a rough day?"

"You could say that."

"I calculated he would. Here's a blanket. I was sworn to secrecy. I cannot tell from whence it came. The idea is that you are getting too soft to sleep in the cold. You've been nursemaided by Doc Smith too long," Jeremy joked.

"What would I do without you, Yank?" John was deeply grateful.

"Probably—" The low, but very distinct growling of John's stomach interrupted Jeremy's lively answer.

"The Falcon flew off before I had a chance to eat," John apologized. John got a glimpse of the redhead's fiery temper. With flushed face and flashing green eyes, Jeremy thundered, "That scoundrel Peterson!" John was sure that the captain would have heard if he had been at the other end of the wagon train rather than just in the next wagon.

"I'll see what I can forage from the mess tent." And Jeremy was gone.

The redhead's temper had cooled when he returned with hot coffee, cornbread, beans, and dried venison.

"Rachael and Bold Hunter send their greetings."

"Um." John was busy eating.

Jeremy began to pry. "I think Rachael still prefers your company to Bold Hunter's," he said slyly.

256

John choked on his cornbread.

Jeremy grinned. His suspicions were confirmed when John asked too casually, "How is Peterson progressing with your sister?"

"Can't tell. Peterson might be special or he might be just one of the herd," Jeremy teased. "Got more soldiers buzzing around Hope than flies around buttermilk in the summer. Dad says chaperoning her is a full-time job. He's getting vexed with her. I think she's just enjoying their attention."

Jeremy sobered when John's face grew dismal. He tried to explain his sister's interest in men. "She spent the last four years in a girl's finishing school in Boston. Wasn't even allowed to meet a man after church, much less have one call on her, so she's making up for lost time. Besides, she doesn't encourage them. She just happens to be the only unattached white woman on the train."

A long silence followed.

"You're not very talkative tonight," Jeremy said at last to break it.

"Sorry, I'm rather tired," John apologized.

"Better get some sleep. I've got guard duty from 8:00 o'clock until midnight. I'll check in on you tomorrow night."

"Thanks, Yank. Looks like it'll be a long, cold night. I have guard duty from midnight until dawn." John's voice was dull.

"What! Graveyard duty with two extra hours? Peterson's a foul player. It would serve him right if my sister did get him in permanent wedlock. Be just what he deserved." John didn't laugh.

After Jeremy left, John squirmed restlessly, searching for a comfortable position. How long had he been lying here trying to sleep? His tense body wouldn't relax. Not having heard Peterson return to his tent, he strained to catch the sound of the captain's boots on the frosty ground.

At midnight a shadowy form nudged John. Unlocking his bracelet, a soldier freed him for guard duty. It was inky dark; John couldn't see his hand in front of his face as he stumbled over buried roots, rocks, and other unseen obstacles. The moon and stars were obscured by heavy black clouds. The air was so cold that his nose started watering. He stomped his feet to get the blood running faster through his chilled body. The silence was eerie, with only the whining of the wind around the sleeping wagons. The measured clomp, clomp, clomp of the two men's feet as they paced along their drudging way sounded like a funeral march.

John walked hunched against the chill air, hands shoved deep into his pockets. Despite the cold, he had to fight off sleep. His head began to nod as he plodded.

Endless minute followed endless minute. Was he frozen in space? Had time ceased to exist? Was he condemned to spend eternity locked in frozen darkness? *This is what eternity will be like for those who refuse Christ—endless, dark, and without hope.*

Eventually the dark became less thick. A new soldier replaced the original one. "Two more hours. I'm bone-weary. Lord, I need that strength You promised." The prayer whirled round and round in his mind, never ending, just spiraling on and on.

The bugle interrupted the spiraling. John had failed to notice the beginning of dawn. He rubbed his tired eyes and said, "Guess I must have been asleep on my feet." He wondered vaguely what he should do now. His eyes felt like they were full of sand. As the guard marched him to Peterson's tent, John stumbled with weariness.

Inside the tent, Peterson was already at the table, writing. His uniform was impeccable. *Had the Falcon gone to bed at all?* John wondered. The piercing black eyes were inscrutable. *Had he been successful in his campaign?*

"Bring my breakfast immediately," Peterson commanded. The feathered quill scratching on the linen paper echoed his strident voice.

It took a minute for the command to penetrate John's numbed mind.

"What's the problem, Indian? Don't you understand English?" Peterson's voice stung him into action. He blundered to the mess tent.

Once inside, he helped himself to a bowl of mush and a few rashers of bacon while the sympathetic cook prepared Peterson's tray. John's hands trembled from cold and weariness as he set the tray in front of Peterson.

"Clumsy fool! You spilled my coffee." He glanced into John's bloodshot eyes. "Looks like learning to be a soldier is too much for you, 'breed. You'll never make the grade." John glared his defiance.

"Don't just stand there looking like a drunken sailor. Get to work." Peterson worked John until he thought he would drop. The six-hour graveyard duty was a nightmare of endurance. The free time John got during the day was spent in the supply wagon, his long frame stretched over uncomfortable boxes and barrels in exhausted sleep. But he never caught more than a few hours' sleep; Peterson was careful of that. Always he ate on the run, snatching what he could between jobs, except for supper which Jeremy carried to him nightly, more often than not around 9:30 after his final KP duties.

Jeremy brought word that Hope had accepted Peterson's diamond but wasn't wearing it.

22

John's mind was confused, barely functioning. "Is the bugle sounding taps or reveille?" He concentrated, trying to sort the notes in his exhausted mind. "Reveille. The past six hours had been guard duty then, not just another nightmare. Lost count of the days. This discipline can't last much longer. Neither can I."

John stopped at the mess, scalded his mouth with hot coffee in an attempt to clear his thinking, and then plodded into Peterson's tent. Every muscle ached from constant shivering. His hands were stiff and blue with cold, while his eyes watered from the warmth in the tent. His face was flushed and rubbed raw from the wind.

My imagination's running rampant. Peterson looks like a Falcon perched, ready for the kill, John thought.

Peterson felt that victory was his. The Indian was obviously dead on his feet. He savored the moment, much as another man would savor an excellent dinner. Ross had dared humiliate him in public. Now he leaned back in his chair, reached for his pipe, and performed the satisfying ritual of lighting it. Ross swayed on his feet ever so slightly. Peterson puffed slowly. Ross had completed his discipline with reveille this morning. Obviously he had suffered. Peterson wished he had not made that impetuous wager with his squad. But there it was; he had committed himself. This was his last opportunity to break Ross.

Peterson removed his pipe from his mouth and blew several perfectly concentric rings of smoke. His voice was impersonally cold. "Ross, you're the sorriest excuse for a soldier I've ever encountered. You're clumsy, slow, and a lame-brain. You are never punctual. It was impossible to penalize **you** for all your errors, or you would be standing **guard** duty from now until you are fifty. There's nothing in that half-breed body of yours to make a soldier of. You've confirmed my opinion that Indians are an inferior race."

John's facial expression didn't change. In his daze of fatigue he tried to concentrate on Peterson's voice, but it simply wouldn't register on his brain.

His apparent calmness aroused Peterson's anger. He jumped up, kicked back his chair, and glared up at John.

The anger and hatred in Peterson's eyes had a hypnotizing effect on John. He was a fly before a praying mantis.

Ross was not going to lose his self-control. For the first time the idea illuminated Peterson's mind; he was not going to win his private battle with the young Indian. His black eyes flashed and color

262

flooded his face. His eyes widened until the irises were surrounded by white. "A man doesn't ignore a challenge! Are you man enough to face me?"

Peterson glanced wildly around the room. His white gloves, where—there on the bunk. In his agitation, he slapped John harshly across the face with the gloves. "Now defend yourself!" he screamed.

John faltered backward, then regained his stance. He shook his head slightly, as if trying to clear a fog.

Deep purple spread over Peterson's face. He made a desperate choking sound as though he couldn't breathe, as though he were drowning in his own anger.

"Out! Get out! You are released! Never step foot into my tent again!" His voice was so loud that it penetrated John's consciousness. He left.

Movement and the cold air awakened John from his daze. He was mildly surprised to find the fat cook looking at him with admiration.

"Indian, that's the smartest move you ever made. I saw the whole thing. If you had made the least move to strike Captain Peterson, he'd have had you behind bars before you could say your name. Striking an officer is a grave offense in this man's army."

John decided to leave fast. Retrieving his blanket from the supply wagon, he headed into the cold wind and stumbled back toward his own wagon. He didn't even feel the icy wind grabbing at him.

Bold Hunter and Rachael made room for him in

the wagon. Wedged tightly among the remaining **children,** John sank into exhausted sleep. Occasionally their crying or loud prattling drifted into **his con**sciousness, but not for long. Even when the **jolting** wagon halted for the day, he failed to rouse **until** Rachael shook him awake for supper.

His mind was thick with sleep. Looking over the frosty ground in the early twilight, he fancied that the ancient hills looked like old men covered with white hair.

Wagons circled across the rolling hills. Huddled near each wagon around a blazing campfire with large bowls of *canahomie* and Indian bread, the suffering people strove to survive. His people. Two different worlds, the white and the Indian. He fit into both. Under the cultural differences, beneath the color of the skin, apart from their roles as capturer and captive, they were all human beings. Brown or white, each had needs, hopes, ambitions, desires, heartaches. God was there for any man to choose.

Supper was scant. Fresh meat was still unknown. John answered his friends' questions about the past two weeks with a sluggish tongue. His head feeling as large as a pumpkin, he tried vainly to stiffle a yawn. He was stretching and was about to bid his friends good night when they had a surprise visitor.

John didn't see Hope until she stepped into the circle of light from the flickering campfire. Rachael giggled at the expression on his face. His eyes looked glazed, his mouth hung agape, giving him the distinct expression of a hooked fish.

He leaped to his feet. What was it about Hope that made every sense instantly animated, throbbing at her nearness?

"I came to express my gratitude, Mr. Ross, for saving me from that 'savage animal' in the woods," Hope said pleasantly. "Please accept this gift from Father." John accepted the bundle without realizing what he was doing. Although he felt like dancing a jig, he only permitted himself a quiet smile. Fervently he hoped his real feelings were hidden.

"I was only too happy to be of assistance, Miss Worchester," he said. "If the opportunity should present itself again, I would be most happy to repeat the entire procedure." John's soft drawl was very pronounced as he put special emphasis on the words *entire procedure*.

The preacher's daughter was at a loss for words, but her eyes gleamed impishly in the firelight.

"Should the event reoccur, I feel certain I would not have to be called away by duty in such an untimely way," John continued.

"Hm. Sounds like a mystery. Would you two please explain what you are talking about?" Rachael asked.

For a second John panicked. Hope had a dreadful habit of saying just what was on her mind.

Hope was nonplussed, but her finishing school training came to her aid. "Some other time, perhaps. I must leave now. Father is rather irate with me. It's not proper for me to be walking about at night seeing my own friends, it seems. But I did persuade him to let you come to dinner tomorrow evening." Her look included them all. "We can celebrate. Have you told Mr. Ross the news?"

John was weak in the knees. His heart thumped loudly against his rib cage, and he licked dry lips.

"Thank you, we'd love to come," Rachael answered.

Hope was gone before he could offer to accompany her. He stared after her into the darkness.

"What's in the bundle?" Rachael asked, her voice amused. *Dear John,* she thought, *how hard he had tried to hide his feelings. Perhaps if the meeting hadn't been so unexpected, he would have succeeded.*

As John tore at the paper, he felt warmth in his cold hands. A white mackinaw! The desperate problem of how to survive in the steadily dropping temperature was solved for him, but what about the hundreds like him with no coat? Quickly he buttoned out the biting wind. The coat was a good fit, just a bit snug in the shoulders. He had almost forgotten how it felt to be warm. At least the people in his wagon would not freeze. Rachael had managed to sew a full-length deerskin covering from their catch, and Bold Hunter had the wildcat pelt draped around his large frame. The children shared the two blankets and the shawl left by Mrs. Ross.

"Is there something to celebrate?" John asked

to divert Rachael from her fixed gaze on him. She looked like a well-dressed cupid.

Bold Hunter started. Glancing at John from the corner of his eye, he muttered something indistinctly and strode off into the darkness.

Immediately John realized what the celebration was about. "You and Bold Hunter—"

Rachael took one of John's hands and held it in both of her own. Her mouth trembled slightly, and her eyes were very bright. *Thunderation!* John wondered, *Was she going to cry?* He felt a sense of loss, mingled with relief.

"I could never have married you, John," Rachael said. "Since we are of the same clan, we're too close in relationship to wed."

"That would not have stopped me. You know that, Rachael."

John took Rachael's face in his hands, kissing her lightly on each cheek, then tenderly on her lips. "For the beautiful bride."

"We'll name our firstborn son for you," she promised, "John Ross Hunter."

Later, curled close to the campfire, John thought of Hope. There was no question that she was the most physically attractive girl he had ever met. The debonair John Ross vanished, his place taken by a bumbling schoolboy whenever she was near. But what did he know about her? She was brutally frank. She had a temper coupled with a strong will. Obviously she was dedicated to God's will or she would never have undertaken the torturous wagon train to unexplored Indian territory.

From their stolen kiss he had learned she was a girl of hot blood. That was Hope Worchester and he was glad.

She seemed to like him, but realistically, what chance did he stand of courting her?

His mouth tightened. He had no future. No money. Nothing but the clothes on his back, and they had come from her. Suddenly he felt bitter. It was the old bitterness that clamped him like a too tight coat of armor.

"She's got Peterson's diamond too. What does she do, collect men like trinkets for a Christmas tree? The Falcon's caught and so am I. How many others?"

John tossed, unable to sleep.

He woke, touchy and irritable. His friends didn't understand his mood.

"It's a beautiful day, John. The wind is not blowing for once," Rachael said brightly after breakfast.

John scowled at the bright sky, muttering under his breath, "Won't last long. Good things never do."

By midday Bold Hunter had left him to himself.

Rachael finally ordered him back into the wagon for more sleep. That evening while they were walking to the Worchester wagon, he was unusually silent. He dreaded seeing Hope. He wasn't about to be another ornament for her tree.

"John, how good to see you." Pastor Worchester shook hands warmly. He pulled John over to a folding chair next to his by a roaring fire, offered him a hot cup of coffee, and commenced to make him feel like one of the family. Jeremy arrived and stationed himself on John's other side. Rachael went to help Hope. Bold Hunter, grinning happily, stood warming his back at the fire, facing his trio of friends.

John noted how tired Worchester was looking. He had aged greatly during the last month.

"I've been out of touch with the latest news for the past two weeks. Are the people still responding to the Gospel, Pastor?" asked John.

Worchester stared intently at John over the rims of his glasses, his eyes grave. "We're on a one-to-one basis now, son. The only religious service I am permitted to conduct is on Sunday morning. We are quite fortunate that the army does not travel on Sunday. Still, that doesn't come near to filling the need in perilous times like these. As many as ten people are dying daily, and I can't begin to meet the need alone. We still have hundreds of miles to travel, with the worst of winter ahead. This forced removal is beginning to look like the blackest deed the American people have ever committed. The shame of it is that the Indians only desired to be left alone in peace to live their lives out in their homeland." John's face was desolate. "But of course I don't have to tell you two about that."

"Nevertheless," he continued, "the people are turning to Christ in greater numbers then I have ever experienced in twenty years of pastoring.

They have nothing or no one else to whom to turn."

Rachael and Hope appeared with steaming bowls of thick stew. John lost the trend of the conversation.

"Did you hear me, John?" Jeremy questioned again.

"Sorry, what was that?"

"I heard by way of the grapevine that old Chief Junaluska—he saved General Jackson's life during the Battle of Horseshoe Bend—when he saw his people rounded up by Jackson and forced to leave, made a comment." Jeremy stood up. A gifted mimic, he raised his face toward the sky and spoke fiercely, "O my God, if I had known at the battle of Horseshoe what I know now, American history would have been differently written!"

The small group was silent. The moaning of the winter wind was the moaning of the mountain people for their lost loved ones. The grief and loneliness of the displaced people swirled about them like a palpable mist.

Rachael and Hope appeared again with hot bread and coffee.

"You all look much too serious for a celebration," Hope commented. "Dad, can't we liven things up? Why does everyone have such a long face?"

"You're right, my dear. Let us hear your wedding plans, Rachael," The pastor's voice was too hearty.

John felt the conversation move around him, but

he wasn't part of it. He felt like an outsider. His poverty set him apart. He was a man with no future.

Shortly after the meal was finished, a fine-looking young soldier appeared, asking for Hope. John's eyes darkened. Humiliated hurt wrenched his heart. He would avoid Hope. He silently committed himself to his decision. He had nothing to offer her, no knowledge of what his new life would be like or what he would be doing. Besides, he was obviously only a trinket to her. The unknown soldier was probably on the dinner agenda for tomorrow night.

Hope was gone only a few minutes, but John sensed immediately that she was anxious about something. She tried to keep her small face calm, but a worried pucker creased her forehead now and again. She became preoccupied.

"That's right, Dad." Jeremy's voice nudged John's thoughts back to the conversation. "It is up to every Christian on the wagon train to show Christ's love in every possible way. The men in my dragoon have been thinking about what Drowning Bear said. I understand he's a noted orator." He glanced at John for confirmation. "He read a translation of Matthew, but his comment was, 'It seems to be a good Book—strange that the white people are no better after having had it so long.' Then Tom spoke up and said, 'Too bad old Drowning Bear didn't know Jeremy here.' Then they all laughed. Made me pretty uneasy. I don't know if they were joshing or really meant what they said."

271

"Jeremy strong in heart, honorable in tongue," said Bold Hunter.

Jeremy blushed so red that his freckles were no longer visible.

"Many of my people go to place of long rest," Bold Hunter continued. "We pray they go with Christ."

Pastor Worchester led in prayer. The young people rose to leave. John stole a final look at Hope. He'd never noticed that light sprinkle of freckles scattered across the bridge of her nose. Was that preoccupied look an indication that she was still thinking of the young soldier?

"Father, I must speak with Mr. Ross alone," she said. "I will be only a few minutes."

John's heart pounded.

23

"I'm frightened." Hope's voice was only a murmur over the wind which had been steadily rising.

They stood together inside the circle of firelight as the wild night seemed to be trying to drive them apart. She looked like a timid fawn who might run because she sensed danger, but didn't know where to go. The angry wind caught her hair, whipping it around her face.

He yearned to hold her, to protect her, to let her lose her fear in his arms. "Why?" his voice was hoarse with restraint.

She turned her face away. Her small voice was tremulous in the wind. "Matthew Peterson threatened to kill himself."

The words shook John. "Why?" He felt like a parrot. The unnaturalness of the situation held his mind in a net, preventing him from reaching in and pulling out a better response.

"I returned his engagement ring."

Anger sharpened John's tongue. "Why did you ever take it?"

She met his gaze for an instant. John's anger

drained. Whatever she had done, she was having a very hard time telling him. Her look said he should already know the answer.

He tried again. "Why did you take it and then return it?" This time his voice was kinder.

"I—I was afraid if I didn't take the ring, Matt would—" she faltered, then faced him squarely. He had the feeling he was falling deeper and deeper into an irretrievable position. He knew whatever she wanted from him he would give her.

"Matthew had you in his clutches. I was afraid of what he would do to you if I didn't take his ring. I watched him work you day after day when you were obviously exhausted and shaking with cold. I couldn't send you the coat; he would have known it came from me."

John felt hot all over. What was she saying?

"Matt suspected I cared about what happened to you, so I took his ring, hoping he would be less harsh with you. Then, last night I gave it back." Her look dared him to tell her she had done wrong.

John shoved his hands deep into his pockets. He was breathing quickly, his mind whirling in confusion. He faced the cold blackness of the night. She cared for him. But he cared too much for her to ask her to share his life with its unknown future. He steeled himself with a deep resolve before facing her.

"What do you want me to do?" he asked, almost impersonally. "Did you tell your father?"

"No. I couldn't. He didn't approve of my seeing Matt."

"Jeremy?"

"I couldn't tell Jeremy because he would preach at me, then go blundering over to Matt's tent and get himself in trouble."

"So you came to me, not caring if I went blundering over there and got myself into trouble." John's voice was rough with unspoken hurt.

"If I didn't care, none of this would have happened. But Matt can't hurt you now. You're not under his command like Jeremy. Don't you see? You could keep a watch on Matt. You know his habits by now. If he does anything suspicious to make you think he's going to kill himself, you could stop him." She looked totally chagrined.

But what of Peterson's threat? If the captain saw him lurking about, it would certainly provoke him. Peterson would think more about destroying John than killing himself. Of course Hope was unaware of that threat.

"I don't believe Peterson would take his own life."

"I do," Hope said feverently. "He's very rich, you know. He's never been denied anything in his life."

"I'll watch him," John promised. What else could he do with Hope looking at him that way? "You'd best go in. It's cold out here."

The hurt on her face pierced John, slashing his resolve into a pathetic heap. He stepped toward her, but she was already on her way back to the wagon.

Several days passed before he saw her again. A

275

bitter blanket of snow covered the rolling hills outside Golconda, Illinois. Sleet had fallen before the snow. The wagons lumbered over the frozen ground, creaking and groaning, adding their complaint to the wails of the living for their dead.

The train halted south of the Ohio River near the mouth of the Cumberland River. Each team and wagon had to be ferried across, so temporary camps blossomed on both sides of the river. So did burial mounds.

It was a bleak setting for a wedding.

A small group of friends gathered near the bridal pair's wagon in response to an oral invitation. There was no festive finery or decorations for the occasion. Instead of candles lining the aisle of a church, icicles hung sparkling from the boughs of every tree. Snow-covered bushes adorned the hill where the bride and groom stood. A bright wintry sun appeared just before the ceremony, as though God were giving His blessing. The wind changed. Now it was blowing from the south, a white wind which was said to bring peace and happiness.

Pastor Worchester officiated, with John acting as best man and Hope as maid of honor. John couldn't keep his eyes off her, but she refused to look at him.

The ceremony was brief. Tears filled many eyes as the young couple was united in marriage. Surrounded by death, this wedding became a symbol of the future.

Bold Hunter placed in intricately carved silver wedding band on Rachael's finger. Years before he had observed that Rachael was impressed with the Christian weddings that occurred in the mission. To please her, Bold Hunter had fashioned this band of marriage when he was sixteen and she twelve. He had carried it with him from that day. Today, seven years later, his dream came true.

The Christian ceremony over, the ancient Cherokee rites were fulfilled. Bold Hunter, tall, brown, his face handsome with happiness, offered Rachael a handful of dried venison. The ham of venison normally used was unavailable. This was symbolic of his intent to keep their home supplied with meat from the hunt.

Acting as Rachael's nearest of kin, John gave her an ear of corn. Rachael's hands trembled slightly as she placed the corn in Bold Hunter's. She was signifying her willingness to be a good wife.

Three days of feasting and fun following the ceremony were the Cherokee custom. Of course this was impossible.

John kissed the bride, then shook hands heartily with Bold Hunter. "Welcome to the Wolf Clan. We are official clan brothers now, bound to help and protect each other until we die."

Pastor Worchester commented, "It seems a strange policy for the males to leave their homes and kin to join the wife's. The American custom is rather the opposite."

"Yes. The lineage of chief is also handed down to the chief's sister's son, rather than his own. Uncle John has two sisters who have several sons.

If they should die, their sister's children would be in line for the chieftaincy. The entire heritage of the Cherokee is traced through the woman. Bold Hunter is making a sacrifice marrying Rachael, as she has no family lineage," John said, "although I feel certain there are many others who along with Bold Hunter would not consider that a sacrifice, considering what they are gaining."

"John Ross speak truth. Bold Hunter think brother and wife in Christ more important than clan bonds."

The guests came forward with their blessings and hopes for a long, happy life and many children. Hope disappeared immediately after giving her best wishes to Mr. and Mrs. Hunter, along with a large bag of cornmeal.

The guests did not linger, for the day was far too cold to stand outside the protection of their own wagons. Many were barefoot, and bloody tracks followed them in the snow.

John thought how good a Cherokee hothouse would feel. Each home in Georgia had one. A cave cut into the side of a hill, with wooden benches inside called sofas. The men built red-hot fires and steamed themselves. They were used especially in times of sickness and fever or for sleeping in on cold winter nights.

John looked uncertainly toward the wagon that had been home for the past three months. He couldn't sleep in it now. Since his mother's death, as well as the death of six of the children, he, Bold Hunter, Rachael and the remaining seven children had managed to squeeze into the wagon to sleep. *Now I'm as welcome as a mother-in-law on a honeymoon,* he thought. *I'll insist on sleeping outside next to the campfire. Others do, so I can too."*

Jeremy had missed the wedding because of guard duty. Now he came bounding over the snow like a red-headed rabbit, full of surpressed news.

"Captain Peterson has overstepped himself this time, I think. The entire camp is agog at the news." Jeremy's green eyes were shining with mischief.

"Don't aim the gun without shooting it," John said as lightly as he could.

"He and Hope had a fallout, didn't you know? I think he's trying to make her jealous. He has a Cherokee girl in his tent!"

John passed his hand wearily over his face. "Against her will?" he asked, foreseeing an inevitable confrontation with Peterson.

"Nope! And is she a beauty! Carries herself as regally as the Queen of Sheba."

John threw back his head and laughed. He hadn't laughed so hard since—his memory failed him. The release from his burden of keeping an eye on Peterson coupled with the exquisite vengeance of the Lord made him feel so lighthearted he almost rolled in the snow.

Jeremy grinned, delighted at the effect of his news. "What's so mirthful to thee, blithesome spirit?"

"Peterson's in for a surprise with a Cherokee woman. They have the final word in a family.

279

She'll leave him if he doesn't suit her. There's no divorce; the girl just leaves if he's not everything she wants. Women have complete equality with men. You knew, didn't you, that it is the woman who decides when the warriors go on the war trail? Sounds like Peterson's headed down the war trail and he doesn't even know it!''

With a chuckle, Jeremy answered, ''Peterson might get what's coming to him. This beauty's already got him ransacking the enlisted men's tents for clothes for her people.''

''The Falcon will have his wings clipped now. In trying to save face with Hope, he's fitted himself with a hood and leash. Cherokee women know how to hunt with falcons.''

''I was told that she's a 'beloved woman.' What's that?''

''A 'beloved woman' is one who took her husband's place in battle if he was killed. With her courage she earned the distinction of making future decisions in the rule of the nation. She is welcome in the council house. The 'beloved women' sided with my uncle to avoid war against the Georgians and offered passive resistance. That woman's husband must have been killed during the roundup, since we Cherokee haven't been at war for thirty years or more.''

''How did this girl become a 'beloved woman' then?''

''I don't know. She must have fought the soldiers some way. Maybe she's fighting them another way now.'' He looked meaningfully at

Jeremy. They both laughed. "If anyone deserves a vengeful woman, Peterson does."

"Ho, John, I almost forgot. Doc Smith sent his congratulations to the newlyweds. Said he needed someone to help in the medical wagon with so much sickness and all. Wondered if you'd like to come and help him out." Jeremy added with a twinkle, "Besides, the sly old fox said you'd probably feel embarrassed with your girl friend married to someone else, right under your nose."

John was deeply grateful. He was soon settled comfortably with Doctor Smith. He was practicing medicine on his own as soon as Smith felt he was adequately trained. Smith was one of the new breed of liberal doctors who refused to bleed a patient. He was also strict about cleansing his surgical instruments.

John discovered he had a proficiency for medicine. Smith trained John meticulously during the remaining months on the wagon train. He promised to supply John with all the necessary equipment to practice medicine when they reached the Oklahoma Territory. A gift of the newest medical books would be forthcoming as soon as the doctor was free to send them. Doc Smith was pleased to train John; he had no desire to remain in the unexplored territory.

The future was no longer so nebulous.

The wagon train passed laboriously through southern Illinois. In its wake remained blackened areas from numerous campfires, bloody tracks, and a succession of silent unmarked grave mounds, looking like links in a chain of death.

They reached the mighty Mississippi opposite Cape Girardeau, Missouri. The river was running full of ice, so the train was obliged to make camp on the eastern side until the river became clear enough to cross.

During the first night there, John was up all night again. He had successfully delivered a live baby, with both mother and child doing well. No one else inside the wagon was ill. They had a few blankets plus some coats donated from sympathetic army regulars. John prayed that this baby and his mother would survive, and he was determined to check in daily to keep a close eye on them. Baby Bryce had been hard to lose; he didn't want to face that again.

The joy of a new birth died the instant he stepped outside the wagon. The hair on the back of his neck prickled. Feeling a sense of apprehension stronger than he had ever felt, he shuddered.

John paused at the flap of the medical tent, looking around uneasily. The first touch of color lightened the eastern sky. If his reckoning was correct, this was the first day of the new year, 1839.

Hoping daylight would dispel his uneasiness, he turned to watch the sunrise. As the dawn came slowly over the Mississippi, wisps of mist rose from its surface, giving it an eerie, ghostly look. The weak sun slanted off the ice-bound ripples of the river, revealing how cruelly cold the night had been. Already the wind was whipping across the plains, promising a frigid day.

The lonely sound of the bugle blew the morning awake, but the sleeping forms around the dead campfires did not stir. John rubbed the back of his neck uneasily, a feeling of unreality swirling around him like the mist over the river. The wagons draped in their white shrouds were like so many ghostly ships lost on a pathless sea. Like a moment frozen in time, the eerie silence framed a picture of desolation.

The reality of what had happened—something of which his subconscious was already aware—finally penetrated John's mind. The sleeping Indians beside the dead campfires would never wake. Hundreds had frozen to death during the night.

Bone weary, John was still hacking the snow from the frozen ground late in the afternoon. Here the earth was not red like his native Georgia, but brown and bleak. The task of burying the dead had taken most of the day.

Resting on his shovel while looking at the dormant soil, John felt the seed of a growing conviction, planted when he saw his father die, begin to germinate and sprout. The scene of death he had witnessed today had brought it to fruition. Uncle John had been wrong in his strategy of passive resistance against the removal. The nation should have left voluntarily, resettled peacefully in the new territory, and begun life anew out of reach of the white man whose greed for land and gold was like that of a hungry wolf.

A time must come in the future when white and brown would live together in peace, when the white violators of the treaties or the Indian wars and raids were not so vivid in the minds of both peoples.

Uncle John had been right to fight for the nation in the courts and in Washington; but when the irrecoverable decision had been made for the removal by a far more powerful people, further resistance had been senseless.

To relocate family by family within the time set by the Americans, at a convenient time when children were well, when mothers had borne their babies and families were together, taking their possessions with them in a practical manner, would have been inexpressibly better than this forced march with its aftermath of death.

"Still, through the suffering, anguish, and death of my people, God has been with us," John said aloud. "He permitted the wrong decision of one man because He has given us free wills. Yet, even in the evil situation that decision caused us, He has been here among us, working everything out for our good. Of course the United States must take its share of guilt for their decision to relocate us. Their greed for land and gold, their failure to provide us with the necessities of adequate food and shelter—"

Suddenly John was startled by a flurry of green and red. Then Hope was in his arms, sobbing against his shoulder. Her hands were cold in his, her lovely eyes swollen and red, and her pale skin pinched with cold. Her riding habit was stained and torn with wear, but in John's eyes she was without equal.

"Why Rachael? Oh John, why Rachael?" Her voice muffled against him was full of anguish.

John felt the whys in his own mind crumbling like the dead leaves of autumn into tiny, dry fragments against something grown strong, solid, and unyielding in his innermost self. "I don't know why, but I know God and that is enough." His voice was firm with conviction.

He held her while she sobbed out her sorrow in the circle of his arms. When she quieted, he spoke gently, "Rachael had love enough to give her place in the wagon to a dying child and her mother. Bold Hunter was gone, trying to find firewood. He was almost frozen when he came back at dawn and found her."

"But she had so much to live for! She could have been so much help in the new land. They had great plans of opening an orphanage. Surely she would have been more useful to God alive than dead." Her voice was bitter, her mind frustrated with the questions that had plagued John.

"God's ways are higher than our ways. We comprehend so little with our finite minds, but I'm convinced that Christians whose missions on earth are completed are taken to be with the Lord. He makes no mistakes."

She found comfort in his faith.

"Bold Hunter has accepted her death," John continued. "His greatest regret was that, if he had received Christ years earlier, he and Rachael could have married, escaped to the mountains, and hid in the caves of South Carolina."

"They were in love for such a long time." Hope smiled a tremulous smile.

John put his hand on her slender neck, feeling her rapid pulse as he pulled her face gently toward his own. She let out her breath in a long sigh, and they forgot the world of death for a few minutes.

"I love you, Hope."

"I've been in love with you since the first time I saw you sitting outside the stockade with that rebellious look on your face, listening to my father's preaching. Did you know I asked him to introduce us?"

Spring came early in the year 1839. In March, after six months of grueling travel, the wagon train, still traveling the Old Military Road, arrived in the Oklahoma Territory.

John was driving the medical wagon as they entered the beautiful Elbon Valley between gentle hills watered by five clear rivers. The undulating hills were not the familiar Smokies. John experienced an intense longing for his lost family as he sat in the wagon viewing the rolling hills. He watched the train ahead of him as the thin, bedraggled people entered the new land. These people had been torn from their land and their loved ones,